HE CAME FROM GALILEE

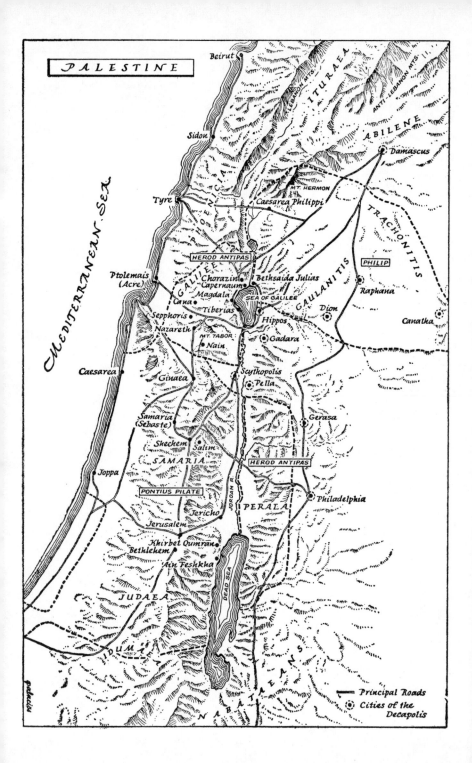

He Came from Galilee

Parker B. Brown

HAWTHORN BOOKS, INC.

W. Clement Stone, Publisher

New York

Library of Congress Catalog Card Number: 73-19385
ISBN: 0-8015-3368-6

1 2 3 4 5 6 7 8 9 10

Dedicated
with gratitude
to
my wife Rosalie
and
daughter Karen Susan

If this is dull, then what, in Heaven's name, is worthy to be called exciting? The people who hanged Christ never, to do them justice, accused Him of being a bore—on the contrary; they thought Him too dynamic to be safe. It has been left for later generations to muffle up that shattering personality and surround Him with an atmosphere of tedium. We have very efficiently pared the claws of the Lion of Judah, certified Him "meek and mild," and recommended Him as a fitting household pet for pale curates and pious old ladies. To those who knew Him, however, He in no way suggested a milk-and-water person; they objected to Him as a dangerous firebrand. True, He was tender to the unfortunate, patient with honest inquirers, and humble before Heaven; but He insulted respectable clergymen by calling them hypocrites; . . . He went to parties in disreputable company and was looked upon as a "gluttonous man and a wine-bibber, a friend of publicans and sinners"; He assaulted indignant tradesmen and threw them and their belongings out of the Temple; . . . He cured diseases by any means that came handy, with a shocking casualness in the matter of other people's pigs and property; He showed no proper deference for wealth or social position; . . . and He retorted by asking disagreeably searching questions that could not be answered by rule of thumb. He was emphatically not a dull man in His human lifetime, and if He was God, there can be nothing dull about God either.

—Dorothy Sayers
in *Creed or Chaos?*

Contents

Preface

Little did I anticipate twelve years ago where the question would lead. In a class in New Testament Greek, the professor inquired if anyone knew how extensive the ties were between the Herods and Rome. "Would someone like to find out for us?" he asked. The subject interested me, so I volunteered.

That project behind me, I continued reading. As I did, a larger world surrounding Jesus came into focus—the Greco-Roman environment of first-century Galilee, about which the Gospels are largely silent. This book is the result of that sustained reading and reflection.

While the last three chapters attempt a partial reconstruction of Jesus' ministry, the primary aim of the book is not that of being yet another "life" of Jesus. It is hoped instead that the book may prove a useful source and guide for those who "would see Jesus" against the full background of His times, which are so like our own.

In writing I have had in mind pastors, religious educators, and college or seminary students. At the same time I have been aware of laymen in and outside the traditional Church who are genuinely interested in the New Testament. For their sake, I have endeavored to clarify terms that may be unfamiliar and have quoted some sources at length. Since certain key articles are available only in technical journals, I have sought to interpret accurately the significance of that published material for a wider lay audience. At different points along the way, therefore, the reader will want to consult notes at the end of chapters. Unless otherwise indicated, biblical references are from the Revised Standard Version of the Bible.

Readers will note that I seem to draw more heavily upon the first three Gospels than the fourth. This is more illusion than fact. The Dead Sea Scrolls and other archaeological finds of the last thirty years have caused a marked change in attitude. No longer is John's Gospel quickly dismissed as more interpretative and less historical than its three companions. For a good summary of arguments in behalf of the Fourth Gospel's reliability, Archibald M. Hunter's *According to John* (Philadelphia: Westminster Press, 1968) is recommended.

"I am a debtor," wrote the Apostle Paul. If he was, I am doubly so, and accordingly take this occasion to thank those authorities who stimulated my reflection and from whose works I have liberally drawn. The conversations I had with Dr. James Rodney Branton of Colgate Rochester Divinity School just prior to his death were most fruitful, and their contribution to my thinking is gratefully acknowledged. I am also indebted to my wife and daughter who, though at times widowed and orphaned by the writing of this book, have never ceased in their love and loyalty toward me. Finally I appreciate greatly the time and thought of those who read and corrected the manuscript and offered suggestions for its improvement: Rabbi Maurice S. Corson, Dr. Arthur F. Carlson, the Reverend William K. Cober, Miss Grace Thompson, and Mrs. Kenneth Medearis.

HE CAME FROM GALILEE

Prologue

"What did Jesus really have to do with such matters?" I asked myself. Vacationing with my family, I sat in church waiting for the sermon to end. The topic, "We Would See Jesus," was interesting, but the sermon was delivering less than it promised, like a balloon I once had, a bright yellow balloon that began the day with a bounce only to lie half deflated and wrinkled by evening.

Perhaps, though, the fault lay not with the sermon but with me. I had other things on my mind. That conversation by the pool for instance . . .

The motor hotel was spacious, its pool clean and inviting. On this particular morning, however, the pool was unoccupied except for two small children, a boy and girl, who splashed in the shallow end. Their mother lounged nearby. In time she and I drifted into conversation, and I discovered she was the wife of a business executive. Her husband, Bob, had brought her and the children with him to Pittsburgh on a business trip. I mentioned some of the attractions of Pittsburgh, but she seemed unimpressed; her thoughts were far away from Highland Park Zoo or the Cathedral of Learning.

Describing the round of cocktail parties she and her husband were expected to attend, she commented, "They aren't that exciting—those parties." The couples invited were always pretty much the same, the atmosphere one of strained cordiality. "I wonder sometimes," she went on. "It's . . . It is all rather boring when you stop to think about it." She stopped again, shrouded in thought. Visibly she shook off what was troubling her and switched the subject. There was more to tell, but not to a stranger.

Over lunch the words of the heavy-set man came to me quick and sharp. He elaborated upon his frustrations: the growing governmental control over his decisions; the complexity of labor relations; the paperwork necessary to conduct normal transactions; the effort to reduce costs and compete successfully with other firms. "I tell you," he snapped, "it's a hell of a way to have to do business!"

The family had moved quietly onto the street earlier that week. The family was black. The street was white. The street was also my own.

As I went to call, the air felt humid. Sunlight breaking through the foliage of tall elms dappled the neat lawns and shingled dwellings around which children normally chattered and ran. It was different now. Maybe the August heat and vacations made it seem quieter.

Still, I wondered. No signs were up yet. I hoped it stayed that way. Otherwise fear would again stampede a community, white residents selling low, black families buying high, and realtors gathering the harvest.

As a minister it was my custom to welcome newcomers to the street, and I saw no reason to make an exception now. The house I stopped at was large and squarish. A blue tricycle sat by the walk leading up to a wide porch. Ringing the doorbell, I waited. Hearing no response, I was pushing the bell again when a youngster came dashing up the drive from the rear of the house. He skidded to a stop in the gravel, his eyes big with surprise.

"Hello," I said, amused.

"Hello," he panted. "I'm Keith. My mother is hanging up the laundry, but she says to tell you she'll be right there."

With that the front door opened, and I was invited in.

The hole in the plate glass entrance of the bus terminal was the size of a man's fist, but I took no special interest in it as I entered the building with my daughter. School was out for the year, and yet the young lady was uncommonly quiet; twelve years old, she was nervous about traveling alone. Like most fathers I was nervous too and therefore overlooked the broken glass on the floor inside.

After purchasing her ticket to Baltimore, we sat down to wait. It was then that I noticed a policeman and a company official examining the damaged doorway. At last they turned in our direction. They walked slowly, their heads down, their conversation subdued. As they passed, enough of their talk reached me to indicate what had happened. The rest of the details I found in the newspaper the next day.

An argument had started about a quarter past eight that morning in a taproom across the plaza. An abusive customer, still carrying his glass of beer, left the bar, with the bartender close behind. The argument resumed on the sidewalk, and the customer suddenly drew a pistol, fired three wild shots, and fled. Getting a revolver of his own, the bartender gave chase across the plaza. Just as his quarry bolted through the terminal's front door, the bartender squeezed off two shots, the bullets smashing the glass and narrowly missing a woman on her way out.

Having seen my daughter safely on the bus, I drove home, studying the sequence of events. Had the bus been scheduled to leave only forty-five minutes earlier, the two of us might have reached the terminal entrance just as the bullets came. "Some world we live in," I thought with disgust. "It's getting so a child can't go to Grandma's on the bus without the risk of being shot!"

By now, at least for me, the sermon was hopelessly derailed despite an aggressive beginning. The minister had opened with a description of Gentile travelers who came to the disciple Philip, requesting to see Jesus. With this as a springboard, the minister stated that if we modern Philips wished to introduce strangers to Jesus in a presuasive way, we must know Jesus firsthand. We ourselves must "see" Him. ("Good," I thought. "That makes sense.") The sermon then sketched in the Jesus we must see and know—a winsome Jesus who used flowers to teach trust in God, a gentle Jesus who enjoyed children, a saddened Jesus who wept over a city, and a compassionate Jesus who healed paralytics. Right now the minister, having joined Jesus in a counseling session with a Pharisee, was calling upon the congregation to be born again. There must be a connection with seeing Jesus, but either I had missed the transition or the minister had failed to provide one.

As it was, my attention was slipping fast anyway. I kept questioning what this Jesus of Nazareth had to do with the problem of gun controls, the exasperation of a businessman who had his fill of bureaucrats and labor disputes, the listlessness of an executive's wife with everything to live with and little to live for, or the razor-edged silence of a street racially invaded. This was indeed some world we lived in, what with social change exploding about us with the fury of a mortar barrage. Where did Jesus of Nazareth fit in? Did He really have any connection at all? Or had the centuries largely dulled the blade of His influence, Church apathy banked the prophetic fire He cast upon the earth, life's modern complexities reduced His "Sermon" to the ineffectualness of an oversimplistic Grecian myth?

My church bulletin slid to the floor and I bent to retrieve it. Its cover featured a biblical scene of frightened disciples rowing through high waves. Behind them a fork of lightning illuminated a misty figure walking on the water. Beneath the picture were the words of the Master, "In the world you have tribulation; but be of good cheer, I have overcome the world" (John 16:33, RSV). The scene was comforting, but also disquieting. Its mood cast Jesus in an ethereal form, pushed Him away, made Him appear distant and obsolete in this Age of Aquarius, air pollution, cybernetics, and future shock. Where was the stout-hearted, sensitive personality mirrored in the Gospels? What had we in the Church done to Him? He was assuredly our risen Lord and Savior, but He was no less flesh and blood before becoming the crystallized subject of creedal affirmations. The indictment voiced by Lewis Mumford was, therefore, accurate: "Little men, who guarded Jesus' memory" had "drained off the precious life blood of his spirit, mummified his body, . . . wrapped what was left in many foreign wrappings, and over the remains erected a gigantic tomb . . . the Christian Church." [1] The situation made me feel like a Mary Magdalene searching under pew pillows and behind altars only to despair. "They have taken away my Lord, and I do not know where they have laid him."

Albert Schweitzer might be right in saying that it is not Jesus as historically known but as spiritually arisen among men who can help our time [2]—but the Jesus of history is not to be ignored either. Christian commitment involves not one but repeated conversions, and among my most transforming moments was that in seminary when a New Testament professor compellingly introduced me to a Jesus I could see and follow. No misty figure in the distance, this Jesus of Nazareth strode manfully down the road to challenge me. He laid claim to me as He had never laid claim to me before. He was audacious. And so was the Gospel which proclaimed Him. What could be more audacious than to announce that in ancient Galilee and Judea events took place which have a direct bearing upon man's current predicaments? What could be more audacious than to see in the child of a first-century peasant woman the missing clue to a life fresh every morning?

"We would see Jesus." Almost twenty centuries have passed since that request was made. And yet the desire to "see" Jesus persists. It is only right that it should, for whenever the Church has advanced some scheme which would reduce the significance of the historical Jesus, the Church has declined. Christianity, after all, is rooted in history. The God announced in the Old and New Testaments acts amid the march and countermarch of historic forces and events. The Savior in whose name the Church is summoned to serve was flesh and blood before He became the subject of theological speculation. Hence Justin Wroe Nixon expressed a timeless truth when at the close of a long and distinguished ministry he declared that "Christianity began with a person. It was because *that person* with his unique quality of life died upon a cross that the Cross has become significant. It is because *that person* rose triumphant over death that Christians are thrilled when they hear him say in the Fourth Gospel, 'I am the resurrection and the life.' " [3]

Of course the warnings of past biblical research must be respected. In the last hundred years alone, ambitious attempts have been made to find the historical Jesus only to fail; efforts by Hermann S. Reimarus, David F. Strauss, Adolf von Harnack, Albert Schweitzer, and Rudolf Bultmann, to name but a few. One must also recognize the temptation to make Jesus in the image of one's desires or religious persuasion, to forget that one's social conditioning, value judgments, intellectual bias, and special interest influence the end result.

Yet, with keen awareness of possible pitfalls, the quest must continue. To not continue is to set aside a pearl of great price worth sacrificing much to obtain. It is only our stained glass windows and tired responsive readings that make Jesus seem so long ago and far away; in reality, human struggles and spiritual achievement across the ages have much in common.

The sermon now finished, the congregation stood to sing. The refrain of the hymn in particular drew my attention.

> I love to tell the story;
>   'Twill be my theme in glory
> To tell the old, old story
>   Of Jesus and his love.

Jesus an "old story"? Not to me. His story mirrors a spirit and commitment unparalleled and unequaled in human experience. Jesus of Galilee an "old story"? Not to those who earnestly ask that they may receive, seek that they may find, and knock that the door of discovery may be open to them.

NOTES

1. Lewis Mumford, *The Condition of Man* (New York: Harcourt, Brace and Co., 1944), p. 63.

2. Albert Schweitzer, *The Quest of the Historical Jesus* (N. Y.: The Macmillan Co., 1948), p. 401.

3. Justin Wroe Nixon, "My Forty-five Years in the Ministry," *Colgate Rochester Divinity School Bulletin,* May 1945.

1 Galilee of the Gentiles

To detach ourselves from accustomed mental images is difficult. Separating us from the Galilean carpenter-turned-prophet are layer upon layer of doctrine and piety. It would appear that everything that could be said has already been said.

One way to break the hold tradition has upon us is to ask a blunt question. For example: How *Greek* was Jesus of Galilee? To some the question is preposterous and unwelcome. If not outright heresy, it smacks of sensationalism. "How Greek was Jesus of Galilee? Why," object these people, "Jesus wasn't Greek at all! He was Jewish." And having rolled a stone across the entrance of that subject, they proceed to other matters, secure in the knowledge that they do not stand alone.

Evidence supporting such a rejection can be quickly marshaled. The Gospels unwaveringly picture Jesus as the product of a devout Jewish family and synagogue. Outwardly He must have looked like any other Palestinian Jew of the time. Male adults wore their hair shoulder length. Combed and parted in the middle, the hair was anointed with a light oil (Matt. 6:17). From the temples, side locks dropped down to combine with mustache and beard in submission to the Mosaic Law. The clothing of Jesus must also have been inconspicuous. A long, sleeveless undergarment was gathered about the waist with a belt. Over this was worn an outer cloak with wool tassels hanging from the corners as required by Deuteronomy. Sandals or shoes protected the feet. In all this Jesus was undoubtedly a conventional Jew, or else we would have heard about it; His critics would have pounced upon any deviation to discredit Him and His message.

Notice, too, that the illustrations of Jesus are of a village-and-country variety. Does not this indicate an individual whose foremost interest and activity lay with simple farm and fishing folk rather than with more urbane and educated residents in nearby Hellenistic centers of commerce and culture? The contacts of Jesus with Gentiles, it may be argued, were at most sporadic and of short duration. According to the Gospels, only on occasion did Jesus venture into Gentile territory (Mark 7:24; Matt. 16:13), and when He did, His object was not a ministry to Gentiles so much as an escape from assassins and a rest from crowds. How Greek was Jesus of Galilee? Not very Greek, it would seem.

Let it be agreed at the outset that in no way are we challenging or de-emphasizing the Jewish ancestry and practices of Jesus when we ask how Greek He was. The issue being raised instead is that of the importance of a non-Hebraic environment that must be considered seriously. This other environment is commonly referred to as "Greco-Roman," a social, political, and cultural milieu regrettably underplayed in most studies.[1] One is subsequently left with the impression that the Gentile-impregnated atmosphere of Galilee had little or no effect upon Jesus. Nothing could be farther from the truth. That Jesus stepped forth at precisely the place He did—"Galilee of the Gentiles" (Matt. 4:15)—deserves being underscored time and again. That Jesus intermingled extensively with non-Jews and was to some degree influenced by them is highly probable.

Edward W. Bauman strikes an illuminating chord when he writes, "Everyone knows that Jesus influenced the world. Few people stop to consider how the world influenced Jesus. We are often told how he made a greater impact on history than 'all the armies that ever marched and all the parliaments that ever sat.' But we seldom hear how his ministry was shaped and influenced by marching armies and political turmoil in his own time. He did not live in a cultural vacuum, but in the midst of a teeming civilization with a long and honored tradition." [2]

By way of corroboration, another observation may be added, this time from the pen of Norman Cousins, editor of the *Saturday Review*. In an article published simultaneously in Jewish and Christian periodicals, he states that "Jesus grew up in Galilee; the difference between the religious environments of Galilee and Bethlehem had considerable importance. Bethlehem was traditional, orthodox, secure. Galilee was deeply religious, too, but it was surrounded by nonbelievers and Gentiles. The contrasting winds were many; they produced a gale of ideas. People were in a mood for reappraisal and self-examination. The atmosphere, if not cosmopolitan, was at least mixed." [3]

As a mixed neighborhood, Galilee was characterized by social and economic prejudice. In present-day America, ethnic diversification produces comparable reactions. Those of differing racial and national origin are brought close together in older city districts. This makes for undercurrents of animosity, uneasiness, and fear. At the same time it also makes for wholesome competition and creativity, as seen in some of the nation's gifted musicians and authors.

Utterly different is the suburban subdivision. Developed in a matter of months, fiercely insulated against "undesirable elements" of the population, these capsulized communities radiate a uniformity of living pattern and attitudes that verges upon moral and cultural sterility. So much is the same—the homes, churches, and schools; the swimming pools, sailboats, and country clubs; the children, toys, and pets. Fathers leave for work each morning wearing much the same suits, carrying much the same briefcases, reading much the same stock quotations.

Now, admittedly, first-century Galilee was not in all respects like the mixed neighborhood cited earlier. Nor was Judea in all respects like the suburban subdivision of today. Nevertheless the analogy is helpful. The percentage of Gentiles living in Galilee was considerable, much higher than to the south. This being the case, two social phenomena most certainly came into play. Because aliens were more common, greater tolerance was shown during relaxed periods of relative peace and friendliness. A Galilean Jew might wonder if the fatherly concern of his God did not extend to his Gentile neighbors as well. The rabbis [4] ruled that Gentile invalids were to be visited and the Gentile poor supported with the Jewish poor. To cheat a Gentile was considered by some a special sin. A spirit of generosity led even to the opinion that "the righteous among the nations [that is, non-Jews] have a share in the world to come." [5] Zephaniah 3:13 extols the virtues of "those who are left in Israel; they shall do no wrong and utter no lies, nor shall there be found in their mouth a deceitful tongue."

By the same token, however, the very nearness and number of Gentile neighbors only intensified Jewish fear and suspicion in times of rebellion and crop failure. Did not the rabbis also warn against trusting foreigners too far? When passing an armed Gentile on the road, let the Gentile pass on your right so as to be prepared to wrench away his dagger if threatened or attacked. In ascending or descending a stairway, keep above the Gentile lest he have the advantage in leaping down upon you. Under no circumstances stoop down in the presence of a Gentile.[6] Beware of employing Gentile midwives. Do not leave a Jewish infant alone with a Gentile nurse; there is always the danger of poisoning.[7] Trust not a Gentile as a supporting witness in a criminal or civil suit; his word of honor is less reliable than that of a fellow Israelite.[8] The stories of Jonah and Ruth might preach tolerance toward foreigners, but negative admonitions were remembered also.

That life in Galilee was linked to non-Jewish elements is

now clear. How did this admixture come about? Like any organism, a mixed neighborhood does not just happen, it is the consequence of earlier occurrences; and Galilee was no exception.

Much as they do today, events in the Near East during ancient times resembled the action of· a chess game. Amid the enervating moves and countermoves of her aggressive neighbors, Palestine [9] became little more than a political pawn. With the death of King Solomon in 926 B.C., the dream of Israel's becoming a secure power faded. Almost at once tribal feuds erupted in open fighting, and the larger realm soon divided into two small kingdoms: Israel in the north and Judah in the south. Save for a few brief periods, the centuries that followed were unstable ones full of military invasions and diplomatic maneuvering. At times only the payment of tribute to foreign despots staved off subjugation and slavery. As it was, the northern kingdom of Israel collapsed in 734–33 B.C., and its southern counterpart, Judah, in 587 B.C. Assyrian, Babylonian, Egyptian, and Persian agression each took its toll of the exposed population.

During the fourth century B.C., the orbit of political and military power shifted westward. Greek culture and ideas came into ascendance with Philip of Macedon, who succeeded in extending his territory southward until he controlled virtually all of Greece by 338 B.C. With this as a base of operations, Philip's son, Alexander the Great, determined to exploit the opportunity to the full. This he did. Winning quickly the allegiance of Macedonia and Greece, Alexander crossed the Hellespont into Asia Minor and within three years totally defeated the armies of Persia. His soldiers then invaded Syria, Palestine, and Egypt, subduing each in turn before pressing on eastward through Asia to India. Wherever this conqueror went, Greek influence and cities sprang up to mark his passing. While later Roman victories were required to consolidate Alexander's accomplishments, the tide of Hellenism was never reversed. This was as true in Palestine as elsewhere.

Alexander died unexpectedly, without designating a successor, and at once his generals fell to quarreling over the spoils. When the dust cleared, two rivals in particular emerged triumphant—Ptolemy Soter, who launched the Ptolemaic dynasty in Egypt, and Seleucus, who, in the north, established the Seleucid dynasty in Syria. Once again tiny Palestine was caught between two great opponents. Fate decreed that it should fall first under the control of the Ptolemies, but this was not to last. In 198 B.C. the Seleucid ruler, Antiochus III, added Jerusalem to his trophies. From then until the arrival of Roman legions, Palestine lay under the shadow of Syria.

The Ptolemies showed religious tolerance toward the Jews' strange practices. The Seleucids, however, did not—an error which in time was to cost them territorially much of Palestine. The policy of the Seleucids was to effect a cultural bond between themselves and their vanquished neighbors. The common denominator in this process was Hellenism. The Jews, though, refused to conform to the all-inclusive pattern of thought and expression. To be sure, some younger Jewish aristocrats spoke Greek fluently, sported heathen garb, and exercised naked in stadiums. But the average Jew did not.

Antiochus IV, called Epiphanes, decided to put an end to such nonsense. Repressive decrees went forth, and soon fires of resistance began to smolder. Angrily the Syrian overlord descended upon Jerusalem. Erecting an altar to Zeus before the Holy of Holies, he ordered pigs slaughtered there. Those who made Jewish sacrifice, practiced circumcision, observed Jewish holy days, or read Hebrew scriptures were put to death. The result was predictable. Revolt exploded throughout the Judean hill country. Ordinarily such a spontaneous rebellion should have been short-lived against seasoned soldiers, but guerrilla warfare and terrorist attacks, then as now, were hard to stamp out. One by one Seleucid contingents were ambushed by the rebels and then repulsed altogether. By December, 164 B.C., Judas Maccabaeus (that is, "the Hammer") led his triumphant army into Jerusalem, cleansed the Temple, and reinstituted proper sacrifice.

One would think that Judas and his followers would have left matters well enough alone, but just the opposite was true. Acting resolutely to entrench the Jews against a Syrian counterattack, Judas marched eastward over the Jordan to rescue patriot families in Gilead from Gentile vengeance. These he resettled near Jerusalem, where they would be safer. His brother, Simon, was dispatched to Galilee for the same reason. Both expeditions were successful.

Small wonder that Galilee greeted the boy Jesus a century and a half later with a racial panorama! Up to the Maccabean revolt, comparatively few Jews had lived in the region. The resettlement of families in the Jerusalem area further thinned Jewish ranks on the frontiers. Later, when Maccabean control reached its zenith under Alexander Jannaeus (103–76 B.C.), steps were taken to repopulate Galilee with Jews from Judea. It is unlikely, however, that these efforts at colonization substantially made up for the earlier loss. One reason was the presence of busy trade routes which kept the land continually open to foreign infection. The numerous Gentiles were also an outcome of military campaigns and occupations.[10] It happens still; people in wartime become dislocated, veterans stay on after discharge or go home and then return. As described by Frederick C. Grant, Galilee was no different.

> In the first century many non-Jews lived there, especially Syrians, Phoenicians, Arameans, Greeks, and Romans. Some of these foreigners were descendants of the peoples who crowded into northern Palestine after the fall of Samaria (in 722 B.C.) or during the period of the Exile (the century or more following 597 B.C.), or during the terrible days of the

Maccabean War. . . . Some were descendants of the veterans of Alexander the Great and his successors, especially of the Seleucid kings, who had been given land and special privileges, such as exemption from taxation, and lived in the Decapolis or "Ten Towns" nearby.[11]

"Galil Hagoyim": the Hebrew means literally "circle of the Gentiles." And a circle it was.

NOTES

1. A notable exception is Frederick C. Grant's *Ancient Judaism and the New Testament* (Edinburgh and London: Oliver and Boyd, 1960).

2. Edward W. Bauman, *The Life and Teachings of Jesus* (Philadelphia: The Westminster Press, 1960), p. 17.

3. Norman Cousins, "The Significance of Jesus as Jew," *United Church Herald,* April 6, 1961, p. 9. Also published in *American Judaism.*

4. The title "rabbi" here and henceforth is used as originally intended: as simply meaning "teacher," rather than in the sense of the highly professional ordained Jewish leader known today. "Rabbinical" will be used in the same manner.

5. Tosefta, Sanhedrin xiii. 2.

6. Avodah Zorah 25b (Babylonian Talmud).

7. Ibid. 25a.

8. Berachot 13b (Babylonian Talmud). The Talmud refers to Gentiles as "a band of strange children whose mouth speaks vanity, and their right hand in raising it to take an oath is a right hand of falsehood." Psalm 144 pleads, "Rescue me from the cruel sword, and deliver me from the hand of aliens, whose mouths speak lies, and whose right hand is a right hand of falsehood."

9. The reference to "Palestine" is acknowledged as not strictly accurate. Gentile rather than Hebrew in origin, the name is derived from "Pleshet" (that is, the Land of the Philistines), that coastal territory occupied by the ancient enemies of King Saul (1 Sam. 17:1). Seafarers trading along the coast evidently used the name "Palaistine" at a later date to indicate the entire country, and the name became commonplace throughout the Greco-Roman world. It is doubtful, though, that the name was used by the Jews. Absent from the Bible, it "is not used in any surviving documents prior to the fourth Christian century" accord-

ing to Samuel Sandmel on page 18 of *Herod; Profile of a Tyrant* (New York: J. B. Lippincott Co., 1967). Its use from time to time in this discussion is thus a concession to reader convenience, since *Palestine* is widely associated with the area occupied by modern Israel.

10. Early in the first century A.D., Strabo, a Greek traveler, compiled a seventeen-volume *Geography* in which he states that numerous Egyptians, Arabians, and Phoenicians lived in Galilee during that period (XVI, ii. 34).

11. Grant, *Ancient Judaism and the New Testament,* pp. 102–3.

2 Crossroads of Crisis

He stood in the doorway examining His injured hand. While constructing a house roof that afternoon, He had been struck by a falling timber. The knuckle, though unbroken, was painfully puffed and discolored.

As if to ease His discomfort, the young builder looked about at the hill country, which rolled away in easy contours. The sun was falling rapidly now, so that shadows already blotted out partially the simple dwellings that overlooked the Plain of Jezreel below. Night had come once more to Nazareth.

He did not need the light to see this land; He could see it in his mind. To the northwest, forests of oak, terebinth, and cypress tumbled down the slopes of Carmel. Behind Him, to the north, Mount Hermon greeted the sky with a summit of snow.

A few hours' walk to the northeast lay the lake. Some days tranquil, some days stormy, the lake constantly fluctuated in color, now jade green, now sapphire blue. Bordered on the north and west by a white collar of towns and villages, the lake was beautiful, its shoreline sprinkled with mimosa, oleander, and jasmine.

On a clear day He could see the rim of the Jordan Valley extending south from the lake. Beyond the valley were the plateaus of Gilead and Moab where forest and pastureland gradually gave way to desert. On a bright morning the view in that direction also included Gentile cities.

Beneath Him a ravine cut its way downhill, its course marked with a path worn smooth by countless feet. At the bottom, where the path emerged upon the plain, a spring supplied water that women carried up in jars.

The Plain of Jezreel itself was a sheet of cultivation stretched westward from the Jordan to the Great Sea. Of all the Promised Land, this region of lower Galilee was most fertile; "milk and honey" flowed here as nowhere else, thanks to better soil and rainfall. Not only the broad plain but the terraced hills were carpeted in yellow, purple, or green depending upon the crop. Grapes, pomegranates, mulberries, figs, dates, wheat, barley, flax—all were there to provide a livelihood for either day laborer or independent farmer. Kitchen gardens, too, were everywhere. Even now their smells reached Him, and He could picture their beans and lentils, onions and cucumbers, lettuce and melons.

The Plain of *Jezreel*—"God sows": the name fit. God had sown liberally, and harvests were good. With twenty years of Roman peace had come a measure of prosperity. Where once battleline had writhed back and forth, swords had clanged, and the wounded had screamed, silence now reigned over the cultivated fields and groves. And yet the ghosts of victor and vanquished lingered on. It was as if the reddish soil had been both colored and enriched by generations of bloodshed. There on the plain His forebears, emboldened by Deborah, overthrew the Canaanite charioteers, a triumph still celebrated in song. There Gideon ambushed and routed the Midianites; Saul perished in battle against the Philistines; and Jehu seized a crown through surprise attacks.

A hyena barked in the distance, its taunting laughter drawing Him back to the present. The stars overhead stood out in the darkness. Had He climbed the slope behind Him, He could have seen the western sea afire in the last rays of the sun. At times the silhouette of a sail was discernable—a grain ship perhaps—or a Roman warship . . .

But He was too weary these days for such excursions. He turned to go in. Night was for rest. Tomorrow would come soon enough.

Galilee as Jesus knew it was the most populous area in Palestine as well as the most fertile. How heavily populated, though, is difficult to determine, due to a scarcity of reliable figures. This was not always the case. During the rule of Caesar Augustus, careful records were kept of census tabulations sent to Rome from all quarters of the empire. This material unfortunately has disappeared, a casualty no doubt of the great fire that later made Nero famous.

We are consequently left to fall back upon statistics supplied by Flavius Josephus. This Jewish commander led rebel forces against the Romans in Galilee about A.D. 66 but espoused the cause of Rome before the revolt was crushed three years later in the south by the brutal siege of Jerusalem and destruction of its Temple. Josephus declares that 204 towns lay in Galilee, none of which had less than 15,000 inhabitants. Now, a total of 3,060,000 people crowded into an area the size of Galilee speaks of considerable density, to say the least, the maximum distance between Galilee's borders north and south being approximately forty miles, and east and west twenty-five miles. Josephus exaggerated. A current authority therefore has set a much lower figure for Galilee—400,000.[1] This he states, however, is a guess based upon factors employed elsewhere in calculating ancient populations.

A cloud of mystery thus blurs the final answer. The best that safely can be said is that Galilee was well populated and in places may have appeared as the "one continuous town" described by a world traveler who studied the region.[2]

Galilee during the lifetime of Jesus was also a maze of roads. In contrast to Judea, whose few roads ran nowhere, Galilee's roads ran in all directions. Leaving Damascus, one roadway entered Galilee from the northeast. Following the contour of the west shore of the Lake of Galilee, this artery wound its way southward until, reaching the port of Tiberias, it turned west. At this point travelers and caravans had a choice of proceeding west along a branch of the road that led to the Mediterranean port of Ptolemais (Acre) or striking southward again past Nazareth to the great coastal highway known as "the royal road" that terminated in Egypt's delta. Another caravan route saved both miles and time: coming south from Damascus, it entered Galilee farther east and swung around the lower end of the lake to join the road just mentioned. The traffic passing near Nazareth was heavy, fed as it was by two Damascus routes.

Nor did these arteries exhaust the road system of Galilee. Commerce and communications demanded additional links, roads south to Shechem and Jerusalem, northwest to Tyre, and west to Caesarea. More than local peasant tracks, these highways were international channels along which sped news of events and scenes far beyond the surrounding plateaus and gorges. Over these highways Gentile peddlers prodded strings of asses loaded with merchandise, their invasion aided by the proximity of heathen cities. The roads felt the tread of humanity in every shape and color: Nabataean camelmen leading their swaying beasts; Jewish families traveling to visit relatives; ebony Sudanese and mahogany Abyssinians bearing the curtained litters of the rich; runaway slaves, secretive and watchful; tax collectors riding in latticed, horse-drawn chariots; tattered beggars clutching empty bowls; imperial couriers with dispatches for commanders in Caesarea or Jerusalem; Babylonian tradesmen bound for Scythopolis wearing elegant silks and nose rings; police patrols returning to barracks at Sebaste; and, of course, farmers with food and hand goods to barter at some town bazaar. The products and wares were as diverse as the travelers. Exported from the region were: wheat, olive oil, dates and figs, honey, balsam, and fish salted in casks for shipment to Alexandria and Rome. Imported were luxury items including: shirts (Cilicia), sandals (Laodicea), baskets (Egypt), basins and pitchers (Sidon), veils and perfumes (Arabia), exquisite dinnerware and pottery (Babylonia), choice wines (India), cheese (Bithynia), and apples (Crete).

The stream of people and products, inventions and ideas could not fail to make an impression upon Jesus as a boy and then as a young artisan. To Him, as to so many children since, Walt Whitman's insight applies:

> There was a child went forth everyday,
> And the first object he look'd upon, that object he became,
> And that object became part of him.

We can be confident that the youthful Jesus was no less aware of the Roman army and its auxiliaries. The sight of mounted officers with crested helmets and wine-colored cloaks served to remind Him that He lived in an occupied country. While not always in sight, the military muscle of Rome was nonetheless within easy reach. Let a Zealot uprising occur, and Roman troops could be on the scene in a short time by means of an excellent road between Caesarea and Tiberias. Ceasarea, in addition to being the capital of Judea and the residence of Pontius Pilate, was the reserve base for army operations throughout the area.

During the rule of Emperor Augustus, three Roman legions were quartered in Palestine. In A.D. 14, with the accession of Emperor Tiberias, this number was raised to four: Legio III Gallica, Legio VI Ferrata, Legio X Fretensis,[3] and Legio XII Fulminata. When the Seleucids a century and a half earlier attempted to suppress the Maccabean revolt, they failed partly because of poor generals and unseasoned troops. Rome did not make that mistake. The legionaries encamped along the coast from Caesarea to Antioch were well-led, battle-tested veterans. Three, possibly all four, of the legions had campaigned with

Julius Ceasar, and one (Legio III Gallica) had also fought the Parthians under Mark Anthony. Since a legion's strength fluctuated between five and six thousand men, the combined force which could be assembled to meet a crisis was at least twenty-three thousand men. In addition, Roman troops were augmented by those under the control of Herod Antipas, the Jewish puppet king of Galilee and Perea. These mercenaries were recruited among the inhabitants around Sebastē in Samaria, since the Jews themselves were exempt from military services.[4] Garrisoned at strategic locations, these native detachments formed a first line of internal security. Such was the might of the empire poised along its Palestinian perimeter, and it was awesome to all but those reckless with patriotism and hate.

Located, populated, and traveled as Galilee was, the military attitude of Rome toward it is predictable. Galilee was pivotal to the empire's eastern frontier. To lose control of Galilee was to have the center drop out of a defense line stretching eight hundred miles from the Red Sea in the south to the Black Sea in the north. At all costs this must not be allowed to happen.

The threat was real. To the east, in a region occupying what is now a large slice of modern Iran, Parthian tribesmen watched and probed the Roman defenses. These enemy forces had been warded off but never totally subdued. In fact, they had invaded Judea but fifty years earlier and plundered Jerusalem.[5] As a foe they were wily and swift, especially the archers mounted on camels and horses. Rather than engage Roman formations at a disadvantage, these fast-riding bowmen charged the Roman flanks, loosing a volley of arrows as they came. They then just as abruptly retreated with a second volley before the Roman archers could get off an effective volley of their own. (From this desert strategy comes the figure of speech "a Parthian shot," used of any sharp remark or gesture made in parting.)

The alertness of the Roman command therefore is understandable and accounts for the savagery with which legions put down Jewish revolts, among them that of Judas of Gamala at Sepphoris when Jesus was a boy.[6] Josephus describes how Judas and his band of renegades staged their abortive revolt in Galilee in A.D. 6, two years following the death of Herod the Great.[7] Storming the palace and arsenal in Sepphoris, they armed themselves and the army that quickly materialized. Learning of the uprising, Quintilius Varus, the Roman governor of Syria, acted at once to stamp it out. Recapturing Sepphoris, Varus ordered full reprisals taken against its Jewish population. Soon the city lay burned and in ruins. The cavalry meanwhile rounded up all Jewish males thirteen years and older and systematically crucified them. The remaining Jews were sold into slavery.

It is difficult to grasp now the magnitude of such destruction and carnage. Picture hundreds of crosses lining the roads like so many sawed-off telephone poles, each with its moaning, tormented burden! No parents in Nazareth could prevent curious children learning what had happened. From the crest of the hill above the town, the smoke and crosses stood out clearly. In the streets refugees asked for shelter and described the holocaust in detail. Jesus discovered early the meaning of violence and the horror of revolution.

It is apparent, then, that the threat to Roman domination was as much internal as external. The terrain of Galilee bred a stubborn streak of independence similar to that still found among the crags of Scotland and ridges of Tennessee. Even during periods of relative quiet, brigands lurked in the hills and gullies. Their homes in caves were virtually inaccessible. Out of nowhere they could strike again and again to terrorize and loot a Syrian village across the border, attack a caravan west of Cana, or massacre and strip a Roman patrol south of the lake.

First-century Galilee was a crossroad of crisis. Contrary to what some traditional biographies and paintings of Jesus have intimated, the land was not secluded, isolated, and remote. To grow to maturity when and where Jesus did was to grow at the friction points of life.

NOTES

1. Frederick C. Grant, "Jesus Christ," *The Interpreter's Dictionary of the Bible,* vol. E–J, (New York: Abingdon Press, 1962) p. 878.

2. Sir Richard Francis Burton, as quoted in William Barclay's *Mind of Jesus* (New York: Harper and Brothers, 1960), p. 41.

3. It is interesting to note that this particular legion participated in the siege and destruction of Jerusalem in A.D. 70 and was stationed there afterwards to prevent Jews and Christians from reoccupying the ruins. Vineyard tenders and gardeners still unearth evidences of that occupation, among them little tiles inscribed with the legion's emblems (a galley and a boar) and its number (Leg XF).

4. The Roman concession was due to the Mosaic laws which regulated diet and forbade combat on the Sabbath; these restrictions made the inclusion of Jews in pagan units difficult.

5. The Parthians defeated Roman expeditions several times. The Romans' most disastrous defeat at the hands of these tribesmen was at Carrhae in 53 B.C., when 20,000 Romans were killed, 10,000 taken prisoner, and the eagle standards of no less than seven legions captured.

6. The age of Jesus at the time of the Sepphoris revolt is debatable. Estimates range between five and twelve years old.

7. Flavius Josephus, *Complete Works of Flavius Josephus,* Whiston Edition (Grand Rapids, Mi.: Kregel Publications, 1970), *Antiquities,* 17.10.5.

3 That Fox, Herod

The Gospels seldom mention the Herods, and never in a complimentary light. The Christmas story introduces Herod the Great as a cruel, calculating killer of children in Bethlehem (Matt. 2:1–16). Upon the death of Herod the Great, his will stipulated that his territory be divided among three sons: Archelaus, Antipas, and Philip. To Archelaus went the Jewish throne in Jerusalem, the title of "king," and control of Samaria, Judea, and northern Idumea. Emperor Augustus chose, however, to reduce the title of Archelaus to that of "ethnarch," a prophetic decision as it turned out: Archelaus was not an able politician and was soon in trouble. Complaints continually reached Rome concerning riots in Jerusalem and guerrilla activity throughout the countryside. When word of the Sepphoris uprising arrived, Emperor Augustus had enough. Deposing Archelaus, he named a Roman procurator in his place. (The fifth in the line of these governors was, of course, Pontius Pilate, who sentenced Jesus to death.) Thus, except for Matthew's explanation (Matt. 2:22) as to why Joseph settled his family in Nazareth, the Gospels ignore Archelaus.

Another son of Herod the Great is even more disregarded: Philip, whose realm lay northeast of Galilee. Matthew and Mark place Jesus near one of Philip's cities, Caesarea Phillippi (Matt. 16:13; Mark 8:27), while Mark and Luke mention

Jesus passing through the environs of Philip's capital, Bethsaida, on the upper edge of the Lake of Galilee (Mark 6:45, 8:22; Luke 9:10). Beyond this, no reference is made to Philip's domains.

As for Herod Antipas, the Gospels are understandably more vocal. In accordance with his father's will, Antipas inherited control of the district of Galilee and the less populated district of Perea, which lay east of the Jordan River. We are also told that this Herod imprisoned and later beheaded the cousin of Jesus, John the Baptist (Luke 3:18–20; Mark 6:17–29). Thereafter, when news of Jesus reached him, Antipas fluctuated between curiosity and superstition: "John, whom I beheaded, has been raised," he is reported to have said (Mark 6:16). And finally there is that scene, tucked into the Passion story, in which king and commoner confront one another before the crucifixion (Luke 23:6–12). This completes the list of references.

As for the followers of the Herods, periodic hints are given of conspiracy against Jesus (Matt. 22:16; Mark 12:13), but who these "Herodians" were is uncertain. Luke and John are mute on the subject, and Matthew and Mark ambiguous. The most we can deduce is that a body of Jewish opinion existed which upheld the Herodian dynasty as the only viable solution to the cultural-religious clash which strained the conquered country. The Gospels, compiled years later at a distance from Palestine, are naturally indefinite concerning this aristocratic following.

Judging from such a limited treatment of the Herods, we might suppose them inconsequential to an understanding of Jesus. Herod the Great died while Jesus was a toddler, and Herod Archelaus was deposed soon after. Herod Philip's sphere of influence was limited to his territory. Only Herod Antipas, the Jewish overlord of Galilee and Perea, stands out prominently as a libertine, prophet-slayer, and tyrant whom Jesus is recorded to have dismissed with disgust: "Go and tell that fox, 'Behold, I cast out demons and perform cures today and tomorrow, and the third day I finish my course' " (Luke 13:32). The quotation is admittedly colored by the Church's later resurrection experience, but the female gender of the Greek word rendered "fox" conveys the heat of Jesus' contempt for the puppet of Rome.

The Herods and their supporters were nevertheless part of Jesus' environment socially and politically. The faith of Abraham, Isaac, and Jacob was fighting as much for its survival now as during the oppressive days of the Seleucids. The hated Romans had ensured the country's relative peace and order, but at what a price! How could any earnest Jew feel comfortable in his homeland when an insidious process of assimilation was forever seeking to subvert his traditions, values, and ideals? As stated earlier, not only Galilee but the whole of Palestine rested amid an exciting, colorful civilization spawned by Alexander the Great. The lasting effect of this invasion has been described by Bernhard Anderson thus: "Just as the American visitor to the Middle East today can see signs of the spread of western civilization—for instance, advertisements for Pepsi-Cola, Socony Vacuum, or Hollywood movies—so in the Hellenistic period a visitor to the same area would have found gymnasiums, theaters, stadiums, and so on. Moreover, Greek dress became fashionable, especially among the more well-to-do." [1] Such a spiritual and cultural infiltration the loyal Jew found as difficult to resist as King Canute reputedly found the ocean tide.

The penetration of Greek ideas and fashions varied depending upon the reception given it. The upper strata of Jewish society absorbed Hellenistic ways more eagerly than the lower; but highborn or low, few could totally avoid feeling the effects. The court life of the Herods was more Greek than Hebrew. This, of course, was not the first intrusion of Greek ways. Much earlier, during the pre-Maccabean period. Hellenists were active. The religious and nationalistic revolt of the Maccabees checked the foreign penetration—but only for a time. With the appearance of Roman troops and officials, the march of Hellenism was resumed throughout the Holy Land. From then on, a polarity became ever more visible: a cultural assimilation among the aristocracy fused with political submission of the masses on the one hand and religious devotion and mounting nationalism on the other. These two realities, as the revolt of the Jews in A.D. 70 demonstrated, were incompatible. Nevertheless the Herodians— especially Herod the Great—invested much money and considerable diplomacy striving to reach a workable compromise.

A monolithic view of Palestinian Judaism is thus inaccurate. The Hasidim or "pietists" in Judea could growl against heathenish innovations, and the Zealots or patriots in Galilee against Jewish collaboration with the Romans, but neither wing of the resistance could stem the flood that flowed irregularly but irreversibly through the land. We can only conclude with one current authority that first-century Palestinian Judaism had behind it

> a long period of thoroughgoing Hellenism—modified, but not thrown off, by the revival of nationalism . . . and antiquarian interest in native tradition and classic language (an interest itself typically Hellenistic). As the Greek language had permeated the whole country, so Greek thought, in one way or another, had affected the court and the commons, the Temple and the tavern, the school and synagogue. If there was any such thing, then, as an "orthodox Judaism," it must have been that which is now almost unknown to us, the religion of the average "people of the land." But the different parts of the country were so different, such gulfs of feeling and practice separated Idumea, Judea, Caesarea, and Galilee, that even on this level there was probably no more agreement between them than between any one of them and a similar area in the Diaspora.[2]

Everywhere—Hellenism. At times it shouted its presence in the person of a noisy Corinthian peddler; at times it wooed the eye with the grace of an Ionic pillar. The rabbis who denounced the study of heathen wisdom literature ("Cursed be the man who teaches his son Greek wisdom)[3] were not themselves untouched by the Hellenistic atmosphere that, like an unwelcome mist, seeped through devout doorways. The writings of Homer were familiar to certain segments of the Jewish population. The rabbis may not have quoted directly from the Iliad or the Odyssey, but it was unnecessary to read Homer to know him; even illiterate laborers on the docks and streets could retell Homeric myths to speed a dragging hour. So it is that traces of Homeric myths and phrases crop up in rabbinical literature of the period—the mention of weird centaurs, half-man and half-horse, and of seductive sirens, half woman and half-bird.[4] The Dead Sea Scrolls now make it clear that Greek books were found even in the library of the ultra-conservative Qumran Community.

Further substantiation of the Hellenistic penetration is supplied by archaeological finds at the Beth-Shearim cemetery in lower Galilee. The burial places uncovered there are freely decorated with drawings and at points with statues carved in relief. Most inscriptions are in Greek rather than Aramaic or Hebrew, and some of the Greek inscriptions are common heathen adages like, "Be of good courage, no one is immortal." This being true of cemeteries, it is not strange that synagogues were influenced in construction and decoration. Recent diggings reveal synagogues in which the traditional platform and high pulpit in the center of the assembly floor are absent. The first-century synagogue at Capernaum is a case in point. A reconstruction of it reveals rows of Grecian columns surrounding the study-worship area. There is no central reading pulpit. Attached to the main room is an enclosed court with a modest pool. The synagogues of the period also exhibit a "use of animal and human forms in high relief, and tell us that the human and, sometimes, the animal forms were later chipped away, but carefully, so that the rest of the carving would not be damaged."[5] In several synagogues philhellenes even went so far as to include the symbol of the pagan sun god in mosaic floors. What a departure this was from the injunction of Moses against graven images! Once the relaxation of prohibitions against art began it continued, as evidenced by the paintings in the Dura Synagogue.[6] At one time it could be argued convincingly that loyal Jews remained aloof from the Hellenized world surrounding them and knew little or nothing of Greek literature; now this position has been rudely dethroned.[7]

Outside the synagogues, the Jewish aristocracy did not conceal its preference for things Greek. Merchants and landowners, publicans and Pharisees indulged themselves in luxury, their houses designed for the optimum in comfort and hospitality. Where the peasant slept on a thin mat or low frame bed, the wealthy official lounged on a couch set higher off the floor and graced by soft Tyrian pillows and blankets embroidered in gold. Veneered with costly woods or gilded with gold leaf, the couches may even have copied elaborate Roman models in the erotic shapes of female anatomy. Ladies probably imitated the pagan practice of scenting their bedclothes.

Thus on the outskirts of the larger towns a blatant departure from austere Judaism was found, the stone manor houses conspicuous with their arbor gardens, shaded colonades, inner courts, and sumptuous furnishings. The Gospel of Luke mentions Jesus dining at the home of Simon the Pharisee (7:36–38). From the details given, the dinner party was clearly Hellenistic in style, with Jesus stretched out on a low divan eating, like the rest, with His right hand.

Bathing was not new to the Jews; the practice merely became more elaborate and popular under Roman rule. Rabbi Gamaliel used the Roman bath near Acco regularly without any sign of embarrassment, and other cultured, educated Jews frequented the Roman bath adjacent to the pool at Siloam.

The frequency of Greek names is significant. The three sons of Herod the Great bore Greek names—Antipas, Archelaus, and Philip. Of Jesus' disciples, only Judas is purely Jewish in name; the rest have names which are unalloyed Greek or the Hellenized form of an ancient Hebrew name.

As might be expected, foreigners influenced the Jewish populace economically. Roman building techniques were admired and copied, particularly by the Herods in their gargantuan projects. The images of galleys and anchors on Herodian coins shows an attraction to sea trade, though the Jews were not naturally a seafaring people. Local craftsmen, impressed by imported goods, altered their procedures. Native pottery was baked with increasing skill and decorated with white garlands on a black background with contrasting red bands, after the Hellenistic style.

In no area of daily life, however, were foreign ways more evident than in personal attire and grooming. Many Jews in Palestine's middle and lower classes stubbornly resisted the intrusion of Greek fashion; but many did not. The aristocracy, of course, surrendered happily. Like the Herods, the Hellenizers were clean shaven and richly attired. An elegant linen shirt was worn as an undergarment and, on special occasions, elaborate, finely woven robes. Like the nobles of Samaria, the Herodian upper class probably sported finger rings with lovely nude goddesses as well as Judaic religious symbols. Heathen fashion altered women's clothing and hair style. This William F. Albright affirms:

> Clothing and jewellery, hairdressing and other aids to beauty were all assimilated. . . . The dress of the Jew consisted essentially of the same garments, including tunic and mantle, shoes or sandals, and a hat or cap of some kind to protect the head, that were worn by contemporary Greeks. It is entirely erroneous to portray the men of that day as clad in the modern Arab *"qamis"* and *'abayeh,* with a *keffiyeh* and *'uqal* covering the head; the Arab turban and the Turkish fez were equally unknown, though high conical tiaras were often worn by pagan priests of the time.[8]

To what extremes in dress and ornament the aristocracy went we can only suspect. Josephus mentions depraved young men sprinkling their long locks with gold dust to give them added brilliance, and declares that Herod the Great dyed his hair.[9] As for wealthy women, many may have discarded the practice of plaiting their hair in favor of piling it on top of their heads as did the matrons of Rome or Antioch. Nothing was spared in the use of cosmetics—dyes, rouges, lipstick. Women proud of their amorous adventures resorted to borrowing the pagan practice of applying eye shadow to give the appearance of having been awake and occupied all night with a furtive lover. Herodias, who, as the wife of Herod Antipas, was denounced by John the Baptist, was Hellenist to the hilt: Did she appear some morning with the suggestive shadow makeup? . . . We cannot say with certainty, but the supposition is plausible.

The extent to which Herodian society accepted Greek fashion continues to show itself in archaelogical discoveries like the alleged "Salome's Head" displayed today in the Rockefeller Museum in Jerusalem.[10] Uncovered in a Roman wine jar, the miniature sculpture is definitely from the lifetime of Jesus. The cave where an Arab farmer found it lies near the ruins of Machaerus, the fortress-palace of Herod Antipas, in the dungeon of which John the Baptist was beheaded. Carved from white marble and four inches in height, the sculptured head is that of an Herodian princess. Her hair is drawn back beneath a diadem and distinctively knotted at the back of the head, a privilege reserved only for royalty. Earrings complete the image of opulence. Interestingly, the sculptor was neither Roman nor Greek but a native of Palestine, or possibly Syria.[11] How pronounced is the Hellenistic spirit of sensuousness which breathes from this statue! The Herodian class of Jews obviously was not hesitant about ordering such stone portraits of themselves when it suited their whim and fancy, although they probably did not flaunt them.

Against this backdrop of foreign custom and fashion, the life style of Herod the Great and his family was natural. His court was crowded with Greek-speaking parasites, the presence of whom only increased an atmosphere already anathema to the scrupulous of Jerusalem. Among Herod's foremost advisors was a teacher, Nicholas of Damascus, who sought to lead the monarch in a more or less organized study of philosophy, rhetoric, and history. Another honored person was the Hellenized Pharisee, Pellio. Roman officers, Greek and Roman tutors of the royal children, and various visiting dignitaries filled out the throne room assemblies.

It must be stressed, however, that the Hellenism found in Judean circles was not that of early Greece. Trus, Greek was spoken, read, and written as the most pervasive language of the Roman Empire, but the noble and creative tradition that produced Plato and Sophocles was dead, or largely so. A moral and spiritual decay had long since set in that not even Emperor Augustus could cure with his reforms. Rome might lie many leagues to the west, but the palace life of Herod the Great was no less infected with the perverse practices that besmirched more illustrious courts. Herod had three boy-servants—one to pour his wine, a second to serve his meals, and a third who cared for his bedchamber—and to them all, as Josephus makes transparently clear. Herod was physically attracted by their beauty.[12]

If Herod went to the Temple at times, it was not out of obedience to the Law of Moses or fondness for his Jewish subjects, but for the sake of political expediency. To satisfy Rome, Herod must maintain peace; to satisfy the Jews he must observe some of the outer trappings of Jewish kingship. If abstaining from giving his daughters to heathens in marriage would help keep this delicate balance, Herod would abstain. If exerting influence in behalf of the rights and property of Jews living beyond Palestine would cool revolutionary ardor at home, then Herod gladly exerted such influence in Rome. If erecting a temple in Jerusalem on an extravagant scale would foster the cultural assimilation of the Jews while appealing to their national pride, then the temple would be built whatever the cost. If a delegation of irate Pharisees protested the presence of military trophies in Herod's theater in Jerusalem, Herod could afford to listen to their complaints. Only late in his reign did Herod the Great weary of the double-edged game of wits. An eagle then appeared on his coinage—but by that time Herod was too ill to care much about the religious sensibilities of his subjects.

Free to build much as he wished, Herod amply earned the epithet, "the Great." Over the years awesome structures took shape throughout Palestine, especially around Jerusalem and Caesarea.

Beyond his territory Herod the Great indulged his taste for magnificence even more freely. Citizens at Antioch, Rhodes, and Athens delighted in the public buildings he donated to their cities while at home his over-taxed subjects groaned. Temples honoring Emperor Augustus were everywhere, thanks to Herod's generosity. The list of recipients reads like the index of an ancient atlas: Ascalon (public baths); Berytus and Byblus (city walls); Laodicea (aqueduct); Sidon (theater); Tyre (temple and colonnade); Damascus (gymnasium and theater); Paneas (Temple to Augustus); Rhodes (Temple to Apollo); and Nicopolis, Ptolemais, and Tripolis (gymnasiums): The Romans applauded a builder, so Herod built and kept on building. The Romans admired gladiatorial combat and gymnastic ability, so Herod erected not only gymnasiums but provided exorbitant prizes that made possible the continuance of games in Sparta, Athens, Pergamum, Nicopolis, and Cos. In short, wherever the Olympic action was, there the munificence of Herod the Great was often evident.

We shall not attempt to outline in detail all of the achievements of Herod the Great. We will instead confine ourselves to his building projects at Jerusalem, Jericho, Sebastē (Samaria), and Caesarea, and then look at those of his son, Herod Antipas, at Sepphoris and Tiberias. With the exception of the present Israeli government, these two rulers did more to change the face of Palestine than any others before or since.

"He who has not seen Herod's building has never seen anything beautiful in his life!" [13] How well this general opinion fit the Temple in Jerusalem planned and built by Herod the Great.

During its relatively short span of glory, this architectural extravaganza served to overwhelm Jew and Gentile alike with its beauty. The Temple required three generations of laborers to complete it, and at one stage a thousand priests and ten thousand auxiliary workmen were engaged in the creation of both the principle edifice and its acres of supplementary buildings and courts.[14] Begun in 20 B.C., the Jerusalem Temple area was still under construction when Jesus and His disciples visited it a half century later. In all probability the last stages of building were still incomplete when the Zealot revolution of A.D. 70 caused its destruction. Strange irony this. No sooner were the Temple precincts all but finished than battering rams and torches reduced everything to ashes and rubble.

In order to accommodate the Temple, the narrow summit of Mount Moriah ("Zion") was broadened through the laying of an enormous stone platform supported by piers and arches and buttressed with a wall of hewn stone. This platform, approximately a thousand feet square, more than covered the original site of King Solomon's palace. Around the border of the area, row upon row of marble colonnades were placed and then covered with roofs of Lebanon cedar. It was within these porches that open-air schools were conducted. The eastern colonnade was named Solomon's Porch, the southern colonnade the Royal Porch. Together both colonnades constituted the Court of the Gentiles. From this lower level, broad flights of steps ascended to a second hollow square enclosed by another colonnade. This square was divided by a line of columns into the Court of the Women and the Court of Israel. Within it stood the high altar and the main temple structure. The sanctuary, containing the Holy of Holies, measured ninety feet by one hundred twenty. The front of the building, which was T-shaped, extended in two columned wings an additional thirty feet on either side, and rose a hundred twenty feet in the air. Beneath lay a foundation of stone blocks, each nearly seventy feet long and nine feet wide, their outer surface covered with gold plates. The roof was also of gold plate and protected by gold spikes against birds roosting on it. Thus anchored like a jewel in a landscape setting of bronze, the Temple when viewed from a distance "glittered like the sun; and the whole monument, its white stones unweathered, shone like a mountain of snow." [15]

This monument to Herod's pride was also a tribute to his friendship with Rome. How natural, then, that this Temple complex should be of the prevailing heathen architecture, complete with rows of Corinthian columns at every turn. Only the absence of statues of gods and goddesses set it apart from the Acropolis in Athens.

Hellenistic architecture bloomed profusely elsewhere in Jerulem. In the upper city the palace of Herod the Great drew gasps of admiration from visitors. A palace, fortress, and prison combined, the towering stronghold was joined to the Temple area by a thick wall over which armed reinforcements could be sent quickly should a riot break out among worshipers. Herod chose to name the palace "Antonia" after his Roman benefactor, Mark Anthony; and with its beautiful grounds, the palace exuded an atmosphere of romantic ease in keeping with its name. Even Flavius Josephus despaired of being adequate to describe its soaring towers, sumptuous furnishings, and mammoth bedchambers capable of sleeping a hundred guests apiece.

> The variety of the marbles in these guest-chambers is not to be expressed, for the rare kinds are amassed in large quantities. The roofs also were marvellous, both for the length of the beams and the splendour of their adornments. The number of rooms was very great, and the variety of figures about them was prodigious. Their furniture was complete, and the vessels in them were mainly of silver and gold. There were also many porticoes, one beyond another round about . . .; yet all the open courts were everywhere green. There were, moreover, groves of trees and long walks through them, with deep canals and cisterns, which in several parts were filled with statues of bronze, through which the water ran out.[16]

The fact that the water referred to came from hills beyond Bethlehem by way of an aqueduct indicates the lengths to which Herod went to assure green shrubberies all year long.

In his sponsorship of the arts, Herod strove for excellence. While he was not the first to introduce them to Jerusalem, they prospered under his patronage as never before. Within the very shadow of the Temple, he ordered a theater built that could compete favorably with any in the Roman empire. In it was a stage divided into two parts, a lower level for the chorus and a higher level for the actors. Ringing this stage and rising to a great height were tiers of boxes able to accommodate thousands of spectators. Outside were porticoes to give shelter from the hot sun or an unexpected rainstorm. All along the inner wall of the theater hung complete suits of gold and silver armor as trophies. The walls of the building were appropriately inscribed with tributes to Caesar Augustus as an indication of Herod's loyalty. Here on an afternoon the playgoer might find the stage arranged for "Iphigenia in Aulis," the scene being that of a harbor lined with Athenian ships about to sail against Troy. In all likelihood the productions were respected masterpieces by Euripides or Aeschylus or Sophocles.

But what place had such dramatic productions in a city dedicated to the worship of the one true God of Israel? The intermingling of Jew, Greek, and Roman in Herod's theater, while only a short distance away temple sacrifices and prayers were neglected, was a disgrace! It has even been suggested that comedy was included in the selection of plays:

> Did Herod go further? Did he introduce comedy also . . . which professed no higher aim than merely to amuse? Was virtue ridiculed, as in Athens in the person of Socrates, to produce the low laugh of the multitude? Were the gods travestied . . . and religion held up to ridicule and scorn as in Athens, by a Cratinus, a Eupolis, an Aristophanes? By dress, language, and gesture, was modesty put to blush? Or . . . the strains that were

sung, were they not rather those of a Pindar, or an Anacreon, or a Sappho, than of a David? [17]

This conjecture may well lie near the actual truth, especially during the closing period of Herod's life.

There was, of course, Jewish resistance. In one notable instance, ten young Pharisees conspired to assassinate Herod the Great as he entered the theater. An informer, however, revealed the plot, so that the ambushers were themselves ambushed. Their execution swiftly followed. The informer was then torn to pieces by a mob. Recognized by Herod's spies, the ringleaders of this atrocity were in turn hunted down by the secret police, put to the rack, and then executed along with their entire families. So it went—a policy of blood and iron—as Herod the Great acted to consummate a homogeneous blending of Jewish and Gentile customs.

That Herod should construct a hippodrome outside Jerusalem was an obvious development, especially when Herod himself excelled in horsemanship and used the bow and spear with accuracy. On occasion he went so far as to participate in Olympic games in Greece. Nothing pleased Herod more than presiding over an arena full of gladiators. There were also less grim contests to enjoy: wrestling and boxing, foot and chariot races, discus and javelin throwing. In support of this, Herod raised an extensive gymnasium where naked athletes practiced and bathed, much to the disgust of scrupulous Jews. Of such an arrangement at an earlier time, Posidonius, a Syrian philosopher, wrote: "Life is a continuous series of social festivities. Their gymnasiums they use as baths, where they anoint themselves with costly oils and myrrhs. In the *grammateia* (such is the name they give the public eating-halls) they practically live, filling themselves there for the better part of the day with rich foods and wine; much that they cannot eat they carry away home." [18] Though written about a century before Jesus, the quotation characterizes in substance the gymnasium activity still to be seen around Jerusalem in His day.

With the approach of winter, Herod the Great traveled to Jericho, which was located in the tropical climate of Trans-Jordan. This town Herod enlarged and improved to such an extent that modern archeologists marvel at what the uncovered foundations reveal. The resort house was thoroughly Hellenistic. Two colonnaded courts ran up to galleries built into the outside walls to provide a pleasant place in which to stroll and converse. Inside the palatial residence, airy sleeping and dining rooms were set off in a split-level fashion. A small theater offered entertainment. Beyond the house lay a swimming pool (scene of an assassination by drowning) [19] and terraced gardens graced by fountains.

When Jesus passed through Jericho (Luke 19:1), though, the scenery had somewhat changed. Archelaus, the son of Herod the Great, added to the resort accommodations, but the uprisings which brought about his downfall severely damaged a number of the luxurious dwellings. Peasants used what was left as a quarry. Still, the town visited by Jesus thrived amid its fifteen miles of balsam plantations and date-palm groves. Besides numerous flower gardens and waterfalls, Jesus and His followers could not have missed seeing carved into a hillside the amphitheater with its typical arc of white pillars.

To the north of Jerusalem and Jericho, Herod undertook the reconstruction of the city of Samaria in 27 B.C. This former center of Jewish apostasy, John Hyrcanus had destroyed seventy-seven years earlier. When the Herodian construction teams arrived, therefore, they first had to clear the top of the hill of rubble and then enlarge it to accommodate new walls and towers. The heart of the resurrected city became a sacred square, in the middle of which rose a temple dedicated to Caesar Augustus. From it the new city received its name—Sebastē—a Greek adjective derived from the Roman name Augustus. Throughout the city, streets ran Roman-style at right angles, with four houses to a block. A main thoroughfare bordered by colonnades reached from a triple gate through the central square. The hill on which the city was built rose five hundred feet above a fertile plain. Because it was steep at many places, three terraces were dug encircling the hill, each of them supporting porticoes or covered walks lined with pillars sixteen feet tall. Not even the Jerusalem temple area possessed comparable promenades. To Sebastē foreigners as well as Jews were imported, Herod granting them parcels of land surrounding the foot of the hill and extending outward several miles. There amid a carpet of brooks and vine yards Sebastē sat with its temple and porticoes, looking like a modern wedding cake.

Moving northwest from Sebastē to the Mediterranean coast, we come to the prosperous port-city of Caesarea. The locality had not always been prosperous, however. Prior to 22 B.C., only a small town called Strato's Tower existed there. Neglect had permitted sandbars to clog the harbor. Herod the Great set about solving this problem. True, Joppa thirty miles to the south had a harbor, but it was too open to high winds and waves. Joppa was also violently pro-Jewish: any attempt by Herod to convert it into a Roman port would lead to civil disorder—which would displease Rome. No, rebuilding Strato's Tower would be wiser. Just as the Jerusalem Temple symbolized Herod's conciliation of the Jews, so the modern, artificial harbor on the exposed coast would symbolize his partnership with Rome. A cultural window to the West and a commercial gateway to the East, this Caesarea would be.

As it turned out, the project required twelve years of toil. To protect vessels from gale winds, Herod ordered a circular breakwater one hundred feet wide built out into deep water. Even assuming that Roman cranes and stone-moving machines were employed, the effort was incredible. Into water as much as twenty fathoms deep, enormous limestone blocks were dropped, some of them fifty by ten by nine feet in size. The breakwater thus formed held back the sea enabling engineers to dredge the clogged harbor. When the sandbars had been removed, the men constructed a wharf a hundred feet wide. Soon large warehouses lined the wharf, protected from high waves by a wall erected along its length. Into this secure harbor sailed ships from many nations to receive repairs and to load and unload cargo.

A half-moon in shape like its breakwater, the city of Caesarea swept uphill from the harbor, its streets radiating outward like spokes of a wheel. Between the harbor and the rows of stone town houses lay a marketplace and forum. South of where the breakwater joined the shore, an excellent theater and amphitheater stood. Just landward from the amphitheater on a slight rise of ground a temple proclaimed in white marble the supremacy of Augustus. No devout Jew could live comfortably in this place with its headquarters for three thousand Roman troops, its nude statues lining the main streets, and its sounds of unholy activity filling the night air. Only an enlightened Hellenistic Jew could adjust to such alien surroundings, a Jew like Philip the Evangelist (Acts 21:8),[20] who lived in the city for twenty years.

Such was the building style of Herod the Great—massive with an aura of permanence. It was not surprising that one of his sons—Antipas—should seek to emulate him. Like his father, Antipas was a willing admirer of Hellenist ways. In Rome, he studied Latin and Greek, geography, some refined literature, speechmaking, and perhaps natural history. On the ancient exercise field called Campus Martius, he excelled in horsemanship and military arms. What was more predictable than his wish to build?

Machaerus, the fortress mentioned earlier in connection with the "Salome's Head," was rebuilt with the addition of a palace. Also in southern Perea, Antipas rebuilt the fortified town of Betharamphtha, renaming it "Livias," after the wife of Emperor Augustus. During this period Antipas, as tetrarch, turned Sepphoris into his official residence. "The ornament of all Galilee,"[21] the new city was built upon the ruins left from the Zealot revolt put down by Varus. Inasmuch as this city was but an hour's walk north of Nazareth, it is altogether likely that Jesus joined His carpenter father in laboring there upon the aqueduct which carried water to the underground tunnel and open reservoir,[22] or on the amphitheater or hillside theater.

Sepphoris will loom large, then, in our thinking regarding the Hellenized atmosphere surrounding Jesus, and we will want to return to it later. Suffice it to say for now that Sepphoris overshadowed Nazareth and other settlements. In addition to its weaving industry, its court of twenty-three judges, and its Roman arsenal, Sepphoris was the shopping center for the entire region. Because Galileans were notorious for fraternizing with Gentiles, it is not straining the credible at all to conclude that those in adjacent towns worked and shopped in the largely heathen city when it served their economic purposes to do so.[23]

Fine as Sepphoris was, however, it had a drawback, in winter it was cold. Snowstorms, though infrequent, were not unknown. Herod Antipas therefore began casting about for another capital site more suitable to continuous recreation. When in 14 A.D. Tiberius became emperor of Rome, Antipas was presented with an even better reason—what could be more advantageous than a new capital named in honor of the emperor? Thus, four years later, Antipas and his entourage moved to the port-city of Tiberias on the west shore of the Lake of Galilee.

Though smaller than Sepphoris, Tiberias more than compensated for any deficiency in size by its magnificence. Seven hundred feet below the level of the Mediterranean Sea, the locality was blessed by a continuous summer. Just to the south lay the hot springs that the Roman historian Pliny praised so highly for their curative powers. Surrounded by mountains and the lake the city had natural defenses to supplement those of its walls. Once inside, the visitor might think himself in Athens, so Hellenistic was the architecture and organization of the city. The local government was conducted by a senate of six hundred led by an archon and committee of ten. There was a hippodrome and a forum and a temple acropolis looking down upon the lake from the slope above the springs. Only some synagogues interrupted the Hellenistic scene, a futile concession on Herod Antipas' part toward the devout, who would not willingly enter the city. The reason for the refusal stemmed from the uncovering of an old burial ground at the time that the city's foundations were laid. At once the rabbis declared the area unclean, so that Antipas had to populate the city with Jews by force or bribery.

As might be expected, the palace in Tiberias was of the best. Its front was graced with sculptured animals. Encircling the building, colonnades and porticoes once again provided shade, while inside an elaborate system of hot and cold water pipes undoubtedly fed the baths. Again vast marble halls witnessed the bacchanalian feasting of Antipas. Here the nightly spectacle of licentious indulgence played itself out until exhaustion finally silenced the last chortle of sensual pleasure.

With this we close the curtain upon this other world of aristocratic flavor that, as far as we know, Jesus never invaded until His trial. No mention is made in the Gospels of His ever approaching, much less entering, the infamous ciy of Tiberias, even though it was close to scenes from His ministry. Herod Antipas was "that fox" and stayed that fox. He might make an annual pilgrimage to Jerusalem for the Passover and refrain from placing heathen images on his coins, but Antipas fooled no one. Emperor Tiberius and his wife liked Antipas, but officials in the field feared his secret correspondence with Rome. Pontius Pilate placed no confidence in this half-Samaritan hated by the Jews; and as for Vitellius, proconsul of Syria, he referred to Antipas on occasion as being nothing but a "wily sneak."

Jesus need not have been present, however, to know something of this other world of affluence, power, and conspiracy. His eyes furnished Him some knowledge of it, and His ears undoubtedly more. His attitude and consul in regard to it was cautious. "Beware of the leaven of the Pharisees and the leaven of Herod": the remark derives from a tradition much older than the Gospel of Mark where it appears (8:15); it could go all the way back to a primitive Galilean source.[24] The same wariness of government is seen in two other statements that are exceedingly

old, possibly of the same Galilean strain. One is the response of
Jesus to disciples who requested special privileges: "You know
that those who are supposed to rule over the Gentiles lord it over
them, and their great men exercise authority over them. But it
shall not be so among you," (Mark 10:42–43). The other saying
arises from a discussion of John the Baptist: "Behold, those who
are gorgeously appareled and live in luxury are in king's
courts" (Luke 7:25; Matt. 11:8).

Out of the mists of long-ago Galilee arise these intimations of
the Master's distrust of all that was ostentatious and deceitful.
We could wish we had more, but we do not. In the end we find
ourselves returning to His reproach, "that fox." Two words—
but how much in attitude they reveal.

NOTES

1. Bernhard W. Anderson, *Understanding the Old Testament* (Engle-wood Cliffs, N. J.: Prentice-Hall, Inc., 1966), p. 531.

2. Morton Smith, "Palestinian Judaism in the First Century," in *Israel: Its Role In Civilization,* ed. Moshe Davis (New York: Harper and Brothers, 1956), p. 81.

3. TB Sotah 49b; Baba Kamma 82b and Menahoth 64b.

4. For a detailed discourse on the impact of Hellenism upon rabbinical circles, see Saul Lieberman's *Hellenism in Jewish Palestine* (New York: The Jewish Theological Seminary of America, 5711–1950), pp. 100–13.

5. Smith, "Palestinian Judaism," p. 69.

6. This well-preserved synagogue dating from the third century stands in the ruins of the city of Dura-Europos, located between Damascus and Bagdad. Panels in the synagogue walls depict the patriarchs, kings, and prophets of Israel. For a discussion of the relaxation of Jewish stricture on art, see *The Messianic Theme in the Paintings of the Dura Synagogue* by Rachel Wischnitzer (Chicago: The University of Chicago Press, 1948).

7. Martin P. Nilsson states in his *Historical Hellenistic Background of the New Testament* (Cambridge, Mass.: Harvard University Press, 1941), p. 27: "In the first centuries A.D. some rabbis tried to substitute

a more liberal interpretation of the passage in Exodus (XX, 4) from which the prohibition of painted and curved images of living beings is derived. They yielded to the Hellenistic influence. Such pictures were to be seen in Judaea.

"Complete consistency should never be postulated for popular movements. The people adhered to the Pharisees and found their palladium in the Law. In spite of this they were subject to the charm of Greek art and adorned figures and paintings. What we find after the final fall of the Jews must have its origin and its roots in earlier times. The question may be permitted whether a like contradiction existed in other parts of life."

8. William F. Albright, *The Archaeology of Palestine* (Baltimore: Penguin Books, 1949), p. 216.

9. Flavius Josephus, op. cit., *Wars of the Jews,* 1.24.7.

10. The "Salome in Stone" is fully described in Paul Ilton's *The Bible Was My Treasure Map* (New York: Julian Messner, Inc., 1958), pp. 116–26.

11. Ibid. pp. 124–26.

12. Flavius Josephus, op. cit., *Wars of the Jews,* 1.24.7.

13. Baba Bathra 4a (Babylonian Talmud).

14. Flavius Josephus indicates the dimensions of the Temple effort when he states in his *Antiquities* (20.9.7) that just before the procuratorship of Florus (A.D. 64–66), eighteen thousand workmen were thrown out of work by the completion of the Temple complex.

15. Stewart Perowne, *The Life and Times of Herod the Great* (Nashville: Abingdon Press, 1956), p. 140.

16. Flavius Josephus, op. cit., *Wars of the Jews,* 5.4.4.

17. William M. Willett, *The Life and Times of Herod the Great* (Philadelphia: Lindsay and Blakiston, 1860), p. 243.

18. As quoted by Edwyn R. Bevan in *Jerusalem under the High Priests* (London: Edward Arnold, 1918), p. 41.

19. Convinced that Aristobulus II was a political threat, Herod the Great arranged for his rival to be drowned "accidentally" during a swimming party in Jericho.

20. Called "the Evangelist" by Luke, this Philip is not to be confused with the disciple of the same name who was a member of the original Twelve. A deacon (Acts 6:5) like the martyred Stephen, Philip is reported to have been a missionary among the Samaritans (Acts 8:5–13) and to have converted to Christianity a royal Ethiopian official (Acts 8:26–39).

21. Flavius Josephus, op. cit., *Antiquities* 18.27.

22. "It has been maintained with a high degree of probability that 'carpenter' as applied to Jesus meant not simply a worker in wood but one who worked at the building trade in general." (Shirley Jackson Case, "Jesus and Sepphoris," *Journal of Biblical Literature* 45 (1926): p. 18.

23. For an opposing view, the reader is directed to a technical work by Albrecht Alt, *Where Jesus Worked* (London: The Epworth Press, 1961).

24. At this point we are indebted to Sherman E. Johnson for insights in his article "Jesus and First-Century Galilee," in *Memoriam Ernst Lohmeyer,* ed. W. Schmauch (Stuttgart: Evangelische Verlagswerk, 1951), pp. 73–88.

4   Cities Far and Near

For the earnest student of the New Testament, the journeys of Jesus outside Galilee and Judea are puzzling. The Gospel of Mark (the earliest of the synoptics and hence, one might assume, the most clear) leaves the reader mystified with statements like, "Then he returned from the region of Tyre, and went through Sidon to the Sea of Galilee, through the region of the Decapolis" (Mark 7:31). On a map of Palestine, such a line of travel stretches out like an awkward question mark, its period resting on the Mediterranean coast, its rounded head curving down along the opposite side of the Lake of Galilee. This itinerary appears unfinished, its close uncertain—"through the region of the Decapolis." Through to where? For what purpose? We are not told.

Still, tenuous though the Gospel references to the Decapolis may be, they cannot be overlooked. Along with the Herodian cities already described, the cities of the Decapolis fostered the "other world" that swirled about the lives of those who lived and labored in Palestine. Thoroughly Greco-Roman in character, these centers of culture and trade continually made the Jew aware that this land was occupied by aliens and that, furthermore, it lay surrounded by a wider alien world to which many of his countrymen had gone and from which many returned annually at the time of the Passover.

With one exception (Scythopolis), all the cities of the Decapolis stood east of the Jordan River. Far antedating the reign of the Herods, these fortified centers were built and populated by the Seleucid successors of Alexander the Great. With the rise of the Maccabees, however, came hard times. Inasmuch as these Greek cities mounted the fiercest opposition to their revolt, Judas Maccabee and his supporters soon launched a military campaign to remove this source of heathen infection. Later Alexander Jannaeus resumed the policy of Gentile oppression. Jannaeus and his army, however, were never wholly successful in subjugating the Decapolis; while a number of cities came under their control, including Pella, which chose to be destroyed rather than submit, the efforts of the Judaizers to convert by the sword fell short.

Sixty-three A.D. saw the intervention of Rome with the arrival of Pompey. Imagine the scene which followed throughout the Decapolis. Elation everywhere! Recognizing at once the value of these cities in securing the eastern frontier, the celebrated general set about liberating them. The Jews were confined to the Trans-Jordan area and forbidden to interfere with Greek city-life in any way. So long as the Decapolis cities kept order and were loyal to Rome, they, for their part, had nothing to fear. As a consequence they took on new life and expanded dramatically, the retired veterans of Pompey's legions now being added to the descendants of Alexander's troops.

Originally the cities were ten in number, hence the name given them (Decapolis means "ten cities"). About A.D. 77 Pliny the Elder lists the ten as being Damascus, Raphana, Hippos, Dion, Canatha, Gadara, Scythopolis, Pella, Gerasa, and Philadelphia. Later, though, other lists appear which vary in composition, some new names being added or substituted and some old ones withdrawn. During the second century, for example, the Roman geographer, Ptolemy, cited eighteen cities; later on another writer cited fourteen. Thus the Decapolis was actually a loose confederation of urban centers, their location dictated by commercial and military advantages. Independent in government, each city took Athens as its civic model of democratic rule. Each assumed the hallmarks of Hellenistic organization— temples to Artemis and Zeus, theaters, stadiums, gymnasiums, baths, forums, tombs, gardens, and fountains. Crisscrossing them were characteristic columned avenues periodically interrupted by graceful arches. How pleasant and relaxed life must have been in these cities, compared with the lumbering austerity of native settlements void of beauty and inspiration.

To the Greek, man was created for the city and the city for man, a conclusion summarized by Stewart Perowne. According to him, the city was the second great gift of Greece to humanity (the first being a flexible language). What made the Greek city outstanding was the fact that it was thought a place for enjoyable living.

> Cities there had been before, great and splendid cities like Babylon or Persepolis or Nineveh. But they were rare and special, the capitals of great kings and gods. The idea that every man and woman was entitled to live in surroundings of beauty was absolutely novel. In Syria and Palestine, since the days when the first wall had been built around the first town, in Jericho, six thousand years before Alexander, the city had been a refuge against the enemy, a bulwark and a storehouse, a huddled citadel, to which men resorted in times of trouble, which meant pretty often. The Greeks designed their cities for use and convenience in peacetime. They sited them on plains, by pleasant rivers. . . . As Aristotle put it in a famous sentence (*Politics*, I, 2, 8): "The city was invented to preserve life; it exists to preserve the good life." [1]

Carl H. Kraeling sharpens further the contrast between the new and old concept. The difference he sees as fundamental.

> The agricultural villages and the old cities, which provided little more than crowded shelter for the ordinary inhabitant, reflect the traditional Oriental and prophetic conception that "man is as grass and as the flower of grass." The Hellenized

city and its culture reflect a train of thought that begins with the idea that this is the best of all worlds, that counts on permanence of the world, and that regards it as both the desire and the duty of man to use his reason to achieve here and now a life devoted to and expressive of the highest good. It is obvious that this hither-worldly ideal and the prophetic ideal of the Orient should clash.[2]

As might be anticipated, the influence of the Decapolis "boom towns" was far-reaching. On the west bank of the Jordan, Scythopolis straddled the junction of two primary trade routes connecting Damascus with Egypt. The largest city in the league, Scythopolis held sway not only commercially but religiously over a considerable area, a significant fact when it is realized that only eighteen miles separated it from Nazareth. There, in all likelihood, Herod Antipas openly promoted the worship of Emperor Tiberius as divine, and there the worship of Dionysus, the god of wine, thrived. This latter expression of pagan religion must have been especially repugnant to devout Jews. Where Greece at her best once advocated, "Everything in moderation," this riotous cult with its alcoholic power to lift the worshiper to heights of exultation was marked with everything in excess, as Edith Hamilton has described it: "Drunkenness, bloody feasts, people acting like mad creatures, shrieking and shouting and dancing wildly, rushing over the land in fierce ecstasy." [3]

Also expressive of the "good life" was the worship of Pan, that half-goat, half-man figure whom Greek religion honored as the god of field and forest, flocks and shepherds. To what extent the worship of Pan penetrated northern Palestine is difficult to determine, but there can be no doubt that it existed at Caesarea Philippi at the foot of Mount Hermon. There, cut into a cliff, may still be seen an inscription in celebration of the nature god and his nymphs. Groves of trees, a grotto, and sparkling streams combined to provide a suitable setting.

Then as now, illness and death were daily adversaries. It was natural, therefore, that interest was shown in the healing arts.[4]

At a number of places, the Asiatic Serapis cult was active in Palestine—an Egyptian import. More prevalent, though, was the worship of the Greek god of healing, Asklepios, and of his daughter, Hygieia, the goddess of health. Shrines to these deities were erected wherever hot springs promised relief from pain or mountain breezes cleared the head and lungs. One famous asklepieion was located at Sidon, another at Tiberias on the Lake of Galilee. Maladies reported cured were ulcers, lameness, blindness, pockmarks, migraine headaches, and paralysis. Cleansing themselves ritually, pilgrims would enter the porticoes of the asklepieia in which slithered harmless serpents whose touch was considered the touch of the god himself. The deity might appear to the patient in his dreams. Or—what is more likely—the priest dressed in serpent costume appeared with instructions that, if carried out, brought relief. No doubt the power of suggestion played a substantial role in effecting cures. Asklepios was thus very popular and highly sought after as "the one who leads and controls all things, the savior of the world, the guardian of mortals." [5]

How extensive were the contacts of Jesus with paganism beyond His homeland? In the vicinity of Sidon, did He meet devotees of Dionysus? Did He pass by the sacred groves at Caesarea Philippi dedicated to the god Pan? Did Jesus, upon crossing the Lake of Galilee and landing at Gennesaret (Matt. 14:34), pause to watch pilgrims traveling to the shrine of Asklepios near Gadara? These are tough questions. The very obscurity of the Gospels on such matters makes it difficult to reply with more than conjecture. Look at the evidence.

Beginning with Mark 6:53–56, we read: "And when they had crossed over, they came to land at Gennesaret, and moored to the shore. And when they got out of the boat, immediately the people recognized him, and ran about the whole neighborhood and began to bring sick people on their pallets to any place where they heard he was. And wherever he came, in villages, cities, or country, they laid the sick in the market places, and besought him that they might touch even the fringe of his garment; and as many as touched it were made well." (The substance of this episode is offered in Matt. 14:34–36, though severely abridged.)

In the Gospel of Mark we find further reference to contact with Gentiles. In Mark 3:7–8, Jesus attracts mixed audiences ("A great multitude from Galilee followed; also from Judea and Jerusalem and Idumea and from beyond the Jordan and from about Tyre and Sidon"), while in Mark 7:31, He journeys through Gentile territory from the Mediterranean coast to the "region of the Decapolis." In Luke, no parallel exists to this material, and in Matthew only a general statement, "And great crowds followed him from Galilee and the Decapolis and Jerusalem and Judea and from beyond the Jordan" (4:25).

All three synoptic Gospels agree, on the other hand, that demon possession was healed by Jesus in "the country of the Gadarenes" (the region about Gadara, a league-city of the Decapolis), and that as a direct consequence a herd of swine stampeded and drowned. (This reference to pigs, of course, signifies Gentile territory.) Mark provides this story in lengthy detail (5:1–20); Matthew adds a second demoniac (8:28–34) while again abridging sharply Mark's account; and Luke, for his part, maintains only one demoniac was restored to his senses (8:26–39) and abridges Mark's version but slightly.

Three other incidents remain to be examined: the confession of Peter at Caesarea Philippi, the healing of a Roman centurion's slave at Capernaum, and the conversation of Jesus with a Syrophoenician woman in the region of Tyre and Sidon. Two of the events occur in Gentile territory; the other does not. Yet each shares with the others a theological tendency, its inclusion determined more by doctrinal than historical considerations. Like the Transfiguration story (Matt. 17:1–8; Mark 9:2–8; Luke 9:28–36), also commonly located near Mount Hermon, the account of Peter's confession, "You are the Christ" (Matt. 16:13–20; Mark 8:27–30; Luke 9:18–21), is probably a post-

Resurrection experience read backward into the record because it was inconceivable to the early Church that Jesus' closest friends were unaware during His lifetime of His true identity.

The story of Jesus' healing of a Roman slave (Matt. 8:5–13; Luke 7:1–10; John 4:46–53) is similarly steeped in doctrinal implications. Matthew and Luke acquire it from some source other than Mark, and in each instance the stress is placed upon the faith of the Roman officer rather than upon the healing power of Jesus. The outburst of enthusiasm ("Truly, I say to you, not even in Israel have I found such faith") is one of the rare quotations attributed to Jesus which exhibits a glowing interest in Gentiles. While the saying may be very primitive, one should not lean too heavily on it in support of the idea that Jesus Himself initiated a mission to the Gentiles. This would indeed be snatching at straws, especially since the Gospels of Matthew and Luke date from a period when Christianity had escaped the bonds of Palestinian Judaism and the apostolic mission to Gentiles was in full bloom.

The account of Jesus' argument with a Syrophoenician woman (Matt. 15:21–28; Mark 7:24–30) also presents problems. In the Gospel of Mark, we sense something contrived about the story, in particular its location in relation to events preceeding and following it. The refusal of Jesus to heal a Gentile is odd; only a short time before and again immediately after (Mark 5:1–20; 7:31–37), He is reported to have cured either in heathen territory or amid heathens. It must also be noted that, except for this miracle, the journey was unfruitful. Charles Guignebert calls the account "quite artificial," and judges it to be "probably an allegory designed to show that pagans who believed were admitted to salvation, and has nothing whatever to do with the life of Jesus." [6] At the same time this French authority concedes the strong probability that "some kind of withdrawal out of the reach of Antipas" took place, and that "Phenicia would not have been unappropriate for the purpose." It should also be added that the seemingly contrived or artificial cast to the story may be symptomatic of a narrative pressured and twisted by later church squabbles over the admission of Gentiles to the Christian fellowship. Frederick C. Grant hints at this in his exegesis of the story: "Perhaps a clue to the present form of the story may be found in the saying which Matthew inserts at this point (Matt. 15.24): 'I was sent only to the lost sheep of the house of Israel,' in which the original emphasis lay upon 'lost sheep,' not upon 'Israel'—the meaning would then be: my mission is to the lost and neglected, viz., the Am-haarez, as in Mark 2:17." [7] Whether a mere allegory authorizing the reception of non-Jews into the Church, or a historic fact signifying a missionary interest submerged in the Founder Himself, we cannot be sure.

What conclusions, then, can be drawn? Several begin to take shape.

First of all, Jesus deliberately limited His basic proclamation to His nation. When He came preaching that men must repent for the Kingdom of God was at hand, it was to those whose tradition prepared them for such a message—the Jews. This view is reinforced by the fact that had the Gospel writers been able to present convincing evidence that Jesus ministered freely to Gentiles in Galilee and elsewhere, they would have done so. Part of their intent, after all, was to reach and appeal to an ever-enlarging and enthusiastic Gentile audience. And what of Paul the Apostle? Would he who penned, "For by one Spirit we were all baptized into one body—Jews or Greeks" (1 Cor. 12:13) have missed the chance to strengthen his argument with the example of Jesus could he have done so? To believe this defies logic. This does not mean that the missionary impulse of the early apostles found no impetus in the attitude and actions of Jesus, but simply that such a movement had to await its own fullness of time in the efforts of those who came after.

Second, the record of Jesus' journeys in and out of Galilee argues for a short and harassed career. How else do we account for the erratic shifts of location where Jesus is reported to have ministered? As we have seen, Herod Antipas, like his father, was kept informed by an alert spy network. The resulting atmosphere is felt in this tense excerpt from Josephus regarding Jesus' cousin, John: "Now, when many others came in crowds about [John], for they were greatly moved by hearing his words, Herod [Antipas], who feared lest the great influence John had over the people might put it into his power and inclination to raise a rebellion, . . . thought it best, by putting him to death, to prevent any mischief he might cause." [8] Would Herod Antipas have hesitated, having removed one threat, to remove another? Not likely. So it is we read in the Gospel of Mark this typical entry: "Jesus withdrew with his disciples to the sea, and a great multitude from Galilee followed." (3:7) Only "withdrew"? The translation bears examining. Here, as other places in the synoptic Gospels, the Greek verb translated "withdrew" or "departed" is ἀνεχώρησεν (anechōresen). An example is Matthew's Christmas narrative where the wise men *departed* to their own country by another way" (2:12). Thus the prevalent usage of the word denotes a going back (as in an army retreat) or a going away (as in taking a journey).

Translation, though, must account also for a word's context. What is the context of ἀνεχώρησεν? Looking up primary references [9] to "withdrew" in the synoptic Gospels, we find that seven times out of nine the atmosphere is clouded with danger. In each of the seven instances, withdrawal in response to a threat is strongly inferred.

Fearing Herod Archelaus who rules Judea in his father's place, Joseph withdraws to Galilee with Mary and the child Jesus (Matt. 2:22).

Hearing of John's arrest, Jesus withdraws from the Jordan area to Capernaum in upper Galilee (Matt. 4:12).

When the Pharisees take counsel how to destroy Him, Jesus withdraws from Galilee (Matt. 12:15).

Word of John's execution reaches Jesus, and He withdraws to a deserted place (Matt. 14.13).

Having offended Jerusalem Pharisees and scribes in an argument over ceremonial washing, Jesus again withdraws (Matt. 15:21).

Informed that the Pharisees are plotting with the Herodians to dispose of Him, Jesus withdraws from Galilee to Gentile territory (Mark 3:7).

Being told by disciples of the beheading of John, Jesus withdraws to Bethsaida in the lands of Herod Philip (Luke 9:10).

Because of this reoccurring context of danger, how much more accurate and illuminating it would be in these seven places to render ἀνεχώρησεν as "fled" or "took refuge." Foxes had holes and the birds of the air had nests, but Jesus—hunted throughout the latter portion of His Galilean ministry—had nowhere to lay His head. The common people "heard him gladly," indeed too gladly for His own safety! So, like the prophet Elijah before Him, Jesus scurried off to the protective slopes of Mount Carmel. And with the Galilee-Phoenicia border close by, this would not be difficult. If Mark, therefore, displays a vagueness in detail and confusion in geography, he is to be forgiven. He wrote at a great distance about a land he did not know intimately and a person who did not stay long in one place.

In years to come, the memory of the fugitive experience, of course, faded. That the Lord from Heaven should flee from place to place and hide from His enemies was unthinkable. Thus the adoration of Jesus as the Risen Lord grew and grew with successive generations until the Gospel of John (ca. A.D. 100–110) portrays Him as a fugitive but as the supreme master of all events and circumstances. In this later Gospel the agony in the Garden is omitted. So also is the kiss of Judas, for what god-like personage would be captured and carried off in such an undignified way? No, concluded Christians late in the first century, it was impossible. The Christ had never run away or hid. He had never been surprised, betrayed or overpowered. Instead He had, at the end, gone forth boldly to meet His enemies, identified Himself, and taken charge of His own arrest. To no less than the high priest He had declared, "I have spoken openly to the world; I have always taught in synagogues and in the temple, where all Jews come together; I have said nothing secretly" (John 18:20). In just such a manner, the unwanted memories were undoubtedly rationalized, and the record of them later edited.

Third, the period of time during which Jesus thus hid "over the border" could well represent a sustained exposure to Gentile life. The time-lapse during His wide detour before reentering His native land indicates that His itinerary has been telescoped by Mark. What Mark implies was but a matter of days was probably six or, at the least, five weeks.

This immediately implies, in the fourth place, a more extensive exposure to Gentile society than a hasty reading of the Gospels would suppose, an exposure that has been suppressed. Why this relative silence concerning the travels of Jesus outside Galilee? Christian rivalry would explain it. In Galilee an enthusiastic following of the slain Messiah persisted and, with understandable pride, perpetuated His memory there.[10] In its provincialism, however, this community neglected or ignored the travels of Jesus beyond Galilee. In their present form, the Gospel narratives are dominated by this Galilean strain with the exception of scattered allusions to Gentile retreats and, of course, the Passion story preserved zealously by the Jerusalem Church.

In Jerusalem this latter body of Christians was also disinterested in any flights of Jesus to Gentile districts. Why should the Jerusalem Church be interested, striving as it was for ascendancy over other communities of Christians? Religious prejudice thus invaded the new fellowship, a prejudice Paul had to contend with when later he sought acceptance for his Gentile converts. Perhaps, though, acceptance of outsiders was too much to ask of Jerusalemites; for a long time Judea and Galilee had exhibited an attitude of uneasy truce.

NOTES

1. Stewart Perowne, *The Life and Times of Herod the Great* (Nashville: Abingdon Press, 1956), p. 27.

2. Carl H. Kraeling and Robert M. Adams, *City Invincible* (Chicago: The University of Chicago Press, 1960), p. 196.

3. Edith Hamiton, *The Greek Way* (New York: W. W. Norton and Co., Inc., 1930), p. 294.

4. Two of the best studies of first-century healing practices are Shirley Jackson Case's article "The Art of Healing in Early Christian Times" in the *Journal of Religion* 3 (1923), pp. 238–58; and S. Vernon McCasland's "Religious Healing in First-Century Palestine" in *Environmental Factors in Christian History,* ed. John T. McNeill, Mathew Spinka, and Harold R. Willoughby (Chicago: The University of Chicago Press, 1939, pp. 18–34.

5. Shirley Jackson Case, "The Art of Healing in Early Christian Times, p. 248.

6. Charles Guignebert, *Jesus* (New York: University Books, Inc., 1956), p. 225.

7. Exegesis by F. C. Grant in *The Interpreter's Bible,* vol. 7 (New York: Abingdon-Cokesbury Press, 1951), p. 754.

8. Josephus, *Antiquities* 18.5.2.

9. Consulted are *Nelson's Complete Concordance of the Revised Standard Version Bible* (New York: Thomas Nelson and Sons, 1957), p. 2097; and *A Greek-English Lexicon of the New Testament and Other Early Christian Literature* by William F. Arndt and F. Wilbur Gingrich (Chicago: The University of Chicago Press, 1957), pp. 62–63.

10. I accept here the thesis of Ernst Lohmeyer in *Galiläa und Jerusalem* (Göttingen: Vandenhoeck and Ruprecht, 1936) that two main centers of primitive Christianity existed in Palestine, one in Jerusalem and one in Galilee. This view is contrary to the customary one which holds that no church flourished in Galilee, that the ministry and witness of Jesus there failed, and that His disciples transferred their interest and activity to Jerusalem just prior to or soon after

Pentecost. This popular view, however, does not account for certain inconsistencies, and when probed raises definite problems as seen in the ninth chapter of M. S. Enslin's *Prophet from Nazareth* (New York: McGraw-Hill Book Company, Inc., 1961), pp. 90–97. See also, in this regard, footnote 2, Chapter 9.

5 Family Differences

The differences which separated Jews in Galilee from those in Judea—particularly those in and about Jerusalem—were long-standing. To begin with, Galilee was physically walled off from Judea by Samaria, an apostate district where Jew and Gentile had freely intermarried. While the heretics worshipped the same God as the Jews, revered the same Scriptures, and honored the same lawgiver, Moses, the Jews nevertheless spurned the Samaritans as no better than heathens.

The source of this enmity is found all the way back at the division of King Solomon's territory following his death in 933 B.C. Judah and Samaria immediately began to drift apart. A half-century later, King Omri built the city of Samaria, a political and spiritual rival that mocked Jerusalem until the Assyrians invaded the land. The Assyrians demolished the city of Samaria and settled a mixture of heathen peoples among the Israelites who remained. The new arrivals, unable to master the whole of the Judaic faith, adopted what they could. They accepted the Jewish Scriptures as sacred. Rejected from Temple sacrifice in Jerusalem, the Samaritans resorted to altars of their own, inviting further condemnation and excommunication. What started as jealousy consequently flamed into a hatred that expressed itself in a smoldering barrier of restrictions. Jews were not to travel through Samaria, to conduct business there, or even to converse with the heretics lest defilement result. When Herod the Great erected the Hellenized city of Sebastē on the ruins of ancient Samaria, the construction only confirmed the Jerusalem authorities in their judgment. Thus by the time of Jesus Galileans and Judeans faced each other across a moat of shouted abuse and periodic killings.

The contrast between north and south can be accounted for, secondly, by the history of Galilee itself. As pointed out before, few Jews lived in Galilee before the revolt of the Maccabees. Between 104 and 75 B.C., the Maccabean rulers—notably Aristobulus and Alexander Jannaeus—sought to colonize the area with Jerusalem families, but the effort was never wholly successful. The result was a population so nationally and racially mixed that the more pure-blooded of Jerusalem treated it with patronizing contempt. That "Galilee of the Gentiles" was only tolerably Judaized explains why Nazareth is unmentioned in the Old Testament, the Talmud, or the writings of Josephus. Explained also is the disparagement of Nazareth shown in two proverbs, the first a question: "Can any good thing come out of Nazareth?" (John 1:46); and the second an indictment, "Search and you will see that no prophet is to rise from Galilee" (John 7:52). The latter observation, of course, conveniently brushes over such prophets as Deborah and Elisha. How prejudiced was the Jewish bureaucracy in Jerusalem toward its provincial brethren farther north!

Climate and topography, too, affected outlook and temperament. In the south, Judea stood out as the bastion of faith. Only there could the God of Israel receive proper sacrifice. Only there could the true sons of Abraham hope to dwell undefiled. The arid soil, cut sharply by erosion, bespoke a God jealous of Covenant promises. Even the barley crops clinging to terraced hillsides reflected His proud will. Monotonous as synagogue chants, Judea possessed a certain beauty, but it was a severe, even harsh, beauty.

How different Galilee with its rustling trees, crimson flowers, lush grass, and pleasant streams! The countryside northwest of the lake was so fertile, according to Josephus, that even the indolent felt compelled to rise up and cultivate it.

Bright and active as Galilee was, it was often viewed suspiciously by religious authorities in Jerusalem, and not without cause: Galileans were generally easy-going, freedom-loving, hard to reason with, and frequently pugnacious. They showed a lack of respect for scholarly discussion. The contrasting winds of the northern hill country were indeed many, and produced a gale of ideas. Pilgrims and relatives as well as foreigners flowed through Galilee bearing the strange ways and thoughts of a wider, more knowledgeable world—Babylonia, Assyria, Macedonia, Greece, and Italy. Separated from Judea by Samaria, vulnerable to Gentile culture, the Galilean Jew followed secular and religious customs all his own, some the result of geographic conditions, some transplanted conflicts between rich and poor, learned and illiterate.

The Galilean system of weights and measures was distinctive. The graduated scale was nowhere else in use.

Marriage customs differed between the two regions. In Judea, the bride and groom were permitted an hour of pre-marital intimacy in private before being conducted to the nuptial canopy, whereas in Galilee this privilege was denied. In Galilee, however, the newlyweds were permitted full privacy on their wedding night, which was not allowed in Judea.

Funeral customs differed. Eulogies in Galilee were recited at the house of the deceased before the funeral; in Judea, eulogies were offered at the grave after the funeral. Unlike Judeans, bereaved Galilean families refrained from greeting mourners who visited the home, feeling that such hospitality showed a lack of respect for the dead.

The rights of widows also differed. After the death of her husband, a Galilean widow continued to live indefinitely in the household of her husband, but in Judea it was more likely that after a proper lapse of time the dower fixed by marriage contract would be given the widow in lieu of perpetual care and shelter.

Some differences reflected, of course, no more than a dissimilarity in agriculture. In Galilee, for instance, flax flourished, so that women there, particularly in Nazareth, were noted for producing quality linen. In Judea, though, where sheep-raising was prevalent, women excelled in weaving wool. Besides this, the use of olive oil set the regions apart. While abundant in Galilee, olive oil was a luxury in Judea. So precious was it that the monastic Essenes ruled olive oil a source of defilement if worn as hair dressing.

Every bit as irritating was the Aramaic spoken by Galileans, especially when it fell on scholarly ears. The dialect was distinguishable by its heavy accent and crude burr, and compounding conversational difficulties was the faulty or careless pronuciation of the Galileans. Hence the synagogue elders throughout Judea frequently excluded visiting Galileans from reading Scripture publicly.[1] How could one proud of his Torah learning avoid cringing when a northern provincial ignorantly pronounced "ḥamar," " 'amar," "emar," and "ḥamor" all the same, though the Aramaic nouns meant respectively wine, a garment, a lamb, and an ass!

In view of such social and economic differences, it is to be expected that religious differences were also keenly felt. This is not to imply that no bond existed between the northern and southern Palestinian Jews. There was, according to Morton S. Enslin, in the blood of the Jew, "whether . . . on a Galilean hillside or within the walls of . . . Zion, . . . the steadying confidence that he was not alone but was a part of a people guarded and guided by the Lord God of hosts." [2] True, that steadying confidence did exist. But stubborn differences persisted too, and they ran deeper than the fact that the Galilean peasant, unlike his southern counterpart, refused to light special candles on the eve of the Day of Atonement or to work on the day preceding the Passover festival. On one side of the conflict stood the southern Pharisees, on the other the Galilean country folk, or *'am ha-arez* (literally "the people of the land"). Each of these groups we will want to examine in more detail.

The reader of the Gospels is soon made aware of the Pharisees. Linked with "the scribes," the Pharisees are seen colliding repeatedly with Jesus over some application of the Torah. The bias against the Pharisees in Christian thought has subsequently been strong, and to this day the condemnation of them as hypocrites is apparent in the ordinary definition of "pharisaic." The charge of hypocrisy doubtless stems from the attitude attributed to Jesus in the Gospel of Matthew, the twenty-third chapter. There Jesus castigates the Pharisees for their pretense ("They preach, but do not practice"), their hard-heartedness ("They bind heavy burdens . . . and lay them on men's shoulders; but . . . will not move them with their finger"), their ostentation ("They do all their deeds to be seen by men; . . . love the place of honor at feasts and the best seats."), their religious pettiness ("tithe mint and dill and cummin, and have neglected the weightier matters of the law."), their avarice ("full of extortion and rapacity"), and their spiritual decadence ("like white-washed tombs, which outwardly appear beautiful, but within . . . are full of dead men's bones and all uncleanness"). No less impressed upon Christian memory is the Pharisee who went up into the Temple and prayed thus with himself, "God, I thank thee that I am not like other men" (Luke 18:10–14).

For our purposes here, we will confine ourselves to a limited defense of the Pharisees.[3] Let it be pointed out initially that while Matthew 23 may well contain a deposit of Jesus' criticism, there is a strong likelihood that the chapter is a vast embellishment of the pristine charges. By the time the Gospel of Matthew appeared, the first generation of Christians had passed from the scene; and time, rather than healing the clash between Church and Pharisee, had only served to stoke the fires further. Converts to Christianity were ostracized and expelled from synagogues: they could hardly be expected to praise the virtues of their opponents. To the original charge of hypocrisy were consequently added others, the lengthening list justified by Christian suffering.

That Pharisees did succumb to "the lower passions of hatred and malice and calumny" is indisputable; they were as human as other men. It is equally clear that some were "false Pharisees," for the Talmud itself [4] openly excoriates such. But it does not automatically follow that because Jesus denounced in a parable one Pharisee as hypocritical that He so denounced *all* Pharisees. Neither is it reasonable nor fair to suppose that the proportion of those who betrayed their ideals among the Pharisees was far greater than among Christians. As R. Travers Herford has declared in this connection, "It is a matter of universal experience that in the case of every religion there are some who take it seriously and some who take it lightly, some who are conscious of its inner meaning and some who care only for the outward form. This is quite as true of Christianity as it is of Pharisaism." [5] In view of their primary motives, goals and contributions, then, the Pharisees are deserving of much better treatment at Christian hands than has traditionally been the case.

With this brief apology, we can now look more appreciatively at this religious movement as it forged for itself a lasting place in history. The name "Pharisee" comes from the Hebrew "Pherushim," meaning "separated." Hence the Pharisees were the "separated ones"—separated, that is, from the *'am ha-arez*, whose attitude toward Torah teachings the Pharisees sought to change.

The Pharisees rose to prominence during the Maccabean period. These middle-class laymen and scholars grew extremely influential. They even came to exert political pressure, a number of them by the reign of Herod the Great joining the fanatical Jewish underground. Actually, though, the Pharisees were not a political party, but a rather loose association of religious educators. While from the time of Herod the Great some members drifted toward the emerging Essenes and Zealots,[6] the main body of Pharisees remained intact and dedicated to peace. As before, they devoted themselves to preserving, studying, and teaching the Torah. It was to achieve this that the Pharisees separated themselves from all who were indifferent to the demands of the Torah, whether Herodians who flaunted Hellenistic ways or *'am ha-arez* who ignorantly resisted new interpretations.

Disciplined and aggressive, the Pharisees accomplished much. At their finest they issued what amounted to a revivalistic call to obey God and love His commandments. Prayer, self-consecration and cultivation of the spiritual life greatly concerned them. To these stout soldiers of Judaic faith belongs the credit for developing that effective agency for instruction, the Synagogue.[7] The Pharisees supported the enlargement of the scriptural canon, advocating the addition of the Prophets (200 B.C.) and the Writings (A.D. 90) to the original Torah composed of the Five Books of Moses. While identified most with the local synagogues, they were not indifferent to the manner in which the Temple solidified the national and spiritual aspirations of the Jews. Nor did they oppose the introduction of new festivals —Hanukkah and Purim—which celebrated Jewish victories. The Pharisees approved the hallowing of the Paschal meal and the baptism of proselytes. Unlike the priestly Sadducees who controlled the Temple, the Pharisees speculated about wisdom, angels, and bodily resurrection. They identified with the Messianic hope of Jewish deliverance which excited so many of their countrymen. In short, the Pharisees acted to keep Judaism from becoming outmoded by changing circumstances or subverted by heathen rivals.

Whereas the Sadducees closed their eyes to change and passed out of existence with the razing of the Temple in A.D. 70, the Pharisees survived. From that ruinous Zealot uprising, southern Pharisees straggled northward to Galilee (Tiberias and Sepphoris of all places!), there to make a fresh start. Thus Christianity as well as Judaism owes a substantial debt to these intrepid laymen. In the estimation of one Protestant authority: "Judaism was without a doubt the noblest and purest monotheistic religion in the ancient world; and Pharisaism was its noblest, purest expression—not Sadduceeism, which was ultra-conservative and reactionary; nor Essenism, which was one-sided, pietistic, and semi-monastic; nor Zealotism, which was politically-minded and bent on revolution." [8]

This commendation leads us to inquire what in Pharisaism soured numerous *'am ha-arez*, increased regional tensions, and prepared the ground for an enthusiastic acceptance of Jesus. The Pharisees were innovators. For them, changing social conditions presented a challenge to be overcome rather than feared. In their eyes the Torah was the supreme guide for their nation's actions, the reservoir of all knowledge of the divine will. This was as true for each individual Jew as for the nation as a whole. If the Jews were to become in reality "the People of the Torah," then every facet of their daily occupation must be regulated to show the influence of the Torah and their obedience to its teachings. But how was this to be achieved when much in Jewish society had become drastically altered since Moses handed down the hallowed teachings?

To cope with the crisis the Pharisees reacted in an understandable fashion. Since God had revealed in the Torah all that was necessary for the well-being and happiness of man, what was required were interpreters "who should be able to deduce from what it did say in one case what it would say in another case if it had expressly dealt with that other case." [9] The aim was to turn an antiquated tradition into a living revelation capable of directing every phase of life—home, business, worship, education, hygiene, agriculture, diet, dress, property, and inheritance. To the "Written Torah" was thus appended an "Oral Torah" composed of Pharisaic rulings. Both the primitive material attributed to Moses and these recent "oral" rulings the Pharisees declared to be equally binding. Indeed, the Pharisees believed that the "Shekinah" or Divine Presence directed their efforts to make the desert law applicable to town life and commerce. Like other reformers, they acknowledged that new occasions do teach new duties, that time does have a way of making ancient good at least impractical, if not uncouth.

Their solution, in the main, was therapeutic. To turn back the tide of apathy, the Pharisees studied and taught diligently. Establishing synagogue schools wherever Jews settled, they carried the hallowed truths to the people by means of public reading and exposition of Scripture, their purpose as much humane as pietistic. To lift legalistic burdens, not add to them, was their hope; to clarify the will of God, not obscure it; to simplify holy law, not complicate it. How confusing, for example, was the fourth commandment in the Decalogue: "Remember the sabbath day, to keep it holy. Six days you shall labor, and do work; but the seventh day is a sabbath to the Lord your God; in it you shall not do any work" (Exod. 20:8–10) But what precisely was work, and what was not? The Torah did not specify, and so rulings had to be made in a number of situations. Could an egg laid on the Sabbath be eaten? Was it lawful to keep food warm by the family fire on the Sabbath? Could a farmer or shepherd help an ailing or injured animal on the Sabbath? Troublesome to tradesmen was the requirement that every man remain "in his place" on the seventh day (Exod. 16:29). What was meant by "place"? The Pharisees decided that "place" referred to a city, so that a Jew might cross the length of Jerusalem and go an additional mile beyond without transgressing sacred law.

An endless stream of dilemmas was faced and resolved. Was it lawful for one who vowed to abstain from drinking milk to drink skimmed milk? For one who vowed not to eat cooked food to eat a roast? In a two-story dwelling, which family—the upper or the lower—was responsible for replacing the intervening ceiling-floor? Delving into the Torah, the Pharisees arrived at answers.

Devout, humanitarian, well-intentioned though the original Pharisees were, their descendents fell prey to the curse of organized religion; namely, casuistry. Through interminable debates over hairbreadth distinctions, they were prone to lose sight of the weightier matters of justice, mercy, and faith. The outcome was a faith laden with obligations—613 commandments alone—that ordinary Jews found as difficult to satisfy as Gentiles to fathom. Of course many Jews welcomed this highly systematic approach to religious practice with its promise of guaranteed salvation: blessed was the man who delighted in the law of the Lord, and meditated on it day and night; he would be like a tree planted by streams of water which yielded its fruit in season, and its leaf did not wither (Ps. 1). But for all those who rejoiced in the promise, thousands failed to keep up and dropped exhausted by the effort to ritualize life from dawn to dusk.

To make matters worse, time attached to Pharisaic ranks still another curse of organized religion: love of ostentation. It was not unknown for a Pharisee to time his walk so as to be caught in the marketplace at the appointed hour for prayer, in order that his devotions might be seen and admired. Nor was it unusual to see overly large blue holiness tassels dangling from the edge of Pharisaic garments, or extra-wide phylacteries. To suggest that a majority of Pharisees were pretentious would be as unjust as it would be erroneous, but, pride being a seductive wench, a number of Pharisees probably succumbed to her wiles.

How significant it is, therefore, that the Pharisees chose to press their greatest infiltration of Galilee just about the time Jesus emerged into prominence. Significant, too, is the fact that the reception of these lay teachers was at best lukewarm. Rabbinical discourses of a century or so later leave the clear impression that Galilean Jews (the *'am ha-arez*) were by and large non-Pharisaic, and stubborn in debates. By Pharisaic standards, these natives were ignorant, loutish, and vulgar.

But were the *'am ha-arez* only that? On the surface, yes,

many were. But to dismiss them out of hand would be a mistake and over-simplification. Indications are that while some large landowners were numbered among the *'am ha-arez* of Judea and Galilee through their wilful disregard of Torah teachings, the vast majority of the *'am ha-arez* north and south were small freeholders, tenant farmers, tradèsmen, artisans, and fishermen, who "sinned" against the Torah because they could not avoid doing so. For every Jew in Palestine who was upper middle class, hundreds were lower middle class to poor. Taxes—Temple and Roman—were excessive. Many lived on a close margin economically. Should a drought kill the crops, or sickness the breadwinner, a family might never escape the pathetic army of the destitute. In the face of such persistent economic threat, religious ceremonialism wilts. A man upholds what he can and allows to fall behind what he deems impractical or impossible. So it was during the lifetime of Jesus, the average Palestinian Jew being, in Morton Smith's words,

> the *'am ha-ares.* . . . There are any number of passages which in the Mishna and Tosefta seem to take it for granted that the average man passing in the street, the average woman who stops in to visit her friend, or the average workman or shopkeeper or farmer is an *'am ha-ares.* The members of this majority were not without religion. They certainly did not observe some rules laid down by the Pharisees, and at a later period they were said to hate the Pharisees even more than the gentiles hated the Jews; but they had their own synagogues (though the Pharisees said that anyone who frequented them would come to an early death), they kept the Jewish festivals, and they even observed some of the more serious purity regulations.[10]

Without question the majority of the *'am ha-arez* were reverent toward God. As a matter of fact, the most disadvantaged among them feared the anger of God to the point of superstition, convinced that transgression would bring immediate bad luck or death. The *'am ha-arez* adhered, therefore, to the rudiments of the Torah teachings as taught in the Synagogue. They prayed for the coming of God's Messiah, who would deliver Israel from its oppressors. During a pilgrimage to Jerusalem, the *'am ha-arez* observed the purity laws and avoided defiling Temple sacrifice. The Sabbath was for him a day of rest and worship on which his word was to be trusted as on no other.

Thus the failure of the *'am ha-arez* in Judea, Galilee, and Perea resulted not from impiety but from ignorance and social conditioning carried over from previous generations. Why should an illiterate fisherman be concerned about attaching a mezuzah to his door-post or phylacteries to his forehead and hand during prayer? The miniature Hebrew scrolls within such receptacles were meaningless to him. How, too, could a farmer more than guess when priests in Jerusalem announced the beginning of a new month, or avoid heeding pagan taboos ingrained in his class from the days when his forefathers farmed amid worshipers of Baal? [11]

Or how was a builder or a shopkeeper to comply with all the time-consuming rules of ceremonial purity? Most *'am ha-arez* ceased trying, and as a consequence the southern rabbis took radical action. Arbitrarily they drew a fifteen-mile radius around the Holy City beyond which the common people were considered too suspect to be religiously "clean." This made the entire nation—save those in or about Jerusalem—ceremonially impure, a shocking development to contemplate, for an impure Jew contaminated every dish and morsel of food he touched, making normal social relations impossible. It was so easy to become defiled.

> The proximity of a dead body, a cemetery, contact with the carcass of an animal, seminal issue, sexual congress, sitting on a mat previously used by a menstruous woman—these and many other similar "accidents," defiled one. Some of these defilements were removed by the comparatively easy ceremony of ritual bathing, but others required nothing less than a visit to the Temple and the elaborate ceremonies of sacrifice.[12]

This summary supplied by Louis Finkelstein concludes understandingly that since "even a pious peasant could hardly be expected to undertake the difficult and arduous donkey-ride to Jerusalem whenever he had visited his ancestors' graves or attended a funeral, most of the country population was continually impure." [13]

The continued Pharisaic exhortation on purity and other aspects of the Law therefore must have wearied the everyday Galilean. The smooth urbanity of the southerners galled the northern villager; their friendly overtures and politeness appeared condescending; their passion for learning was mistaken for mere pedantry. The *'am ha-arez* "could not realize that the ease of manner and conversation which was characteristic of the townsmen, as well as their polish and self-control, was so much a part of them as to be almost instinctive." [14]

Over the years this annoyance became deep seated and mutual; the Talmudic discourses of a century or so after Jesus are seared with acrimony. Jerusalem scholars denounced marriages with the unlettered *'am ha-arez*, justifying their position from Deuteronomy 27:21: "Cursed be he who lies with any kind of beast." Rabbi Meir is quoted as saying, "Whoever marries his daughter to an *'am ha-arez* might as well bind her before a lion. Just as a lion tears his victim to pieces and then consumes him, so the *'am ha-arez* beats his wife and then takes her back into his embrace." [15] The vehemence of Rabbi Eliezer ben Hyrcanus is demonstrated by his opinion that it was lawful to stab an *'am ha-arez* on a Day of Atonement provided it fell on a Sabbath, for, said he near the close of the first century, "If the *'am ha-arez* did not need us for the purposes of trade, they would slaughter us." [16]

The *'am ha-arez* replied in kind to such abuse. After forty years as an illiterate shepherd, Akiba (A.D. 50–132) entered a rabbinical academy to become the foremost teacher of his generation. The rise in status, however, did not erase from his memory an earlier hatred: "When I was an *'am ha-arez*, I used to say, 'I wish I had one of those scholars, and I would bite him like an ass.'" "You mean like a dog," corrected a disciple. Undaunted, Akiba explained, "An ass's bite breaks the bone; a dog's does not."[17]

Such samplings of venom measure the heat generated between the privileged and the underpriviliged, the learned and the unlettered, the purist and the impure. The growls of scrupulous Jews swelled at Galilean unwillingness to follow the findings of the new Torah studies. For eighteen years Rabbi Johanan ben Zakkai inhabited the northern hill country; only twice in all that period did the compatriots of Jesus consult him. "Galilee, Galilee," he lamented, "you hate the teaching, and you will end by falling prey to the bandit leaders"—by which he meant the Zealot fanatics—and he was right.[18]

Despite their admitted evangelical bias, the Gospels thus recount with probable accuracy the appearance of emissaries from Jerusalem to test Jesus. Galilee was the mission field of the Pharisees, and they, who would "traverse sea and land to make a single proselyte" (Matt. 23:15), took their duties seriously. It was an exacting, often thankless task. Conformity in doctrine and practice proved difficult to compel. The Galileans refused to observe the Passover on the same day as their Jerusalem brethren. They celebrated it instead on the day before,[19] so that Mark and John in their Gospels are apparently right in maintaining that the Last Supper was a Passover meal observed twenty-four hours before the Jerusalem festival. The Pharisees also held unlawful the Galilean practice of eating dairy products with meat, but Galileans served milk with fowl anyway.[20] In Galilean synagogues the commandment, "You shall not covet" (Exod. 20:17) was replaced in the Decalogue with "Do not defraud" (Mark 10:19), an interesting shift from mere desire to actual cheating, and a substitution in which Jesus apparently concurred.

Independent to the point of obstinacy, the Galilean Jews went about the routine of earning a livelihood, rearing a family and following ancestral customs. No "outsiders" would control their lives simply because they came from Jerusalem or could argue the fine points of Pharisaic theory. Jericho farmers might bow to prohibitions against harvesting grain at a certain time or eating fruit fallen from trees on the Sabbath, but not the Galilean *'am ha-arez*! And out of the midst of these "people of the land" strode Jesus of Nazareth preaching, "The time is fulfilled, and the kingdom of God is at hand; repent!"

NOTES

1. L. E. Elliott-Binns, in his *Galilean Christianity* (Naperville, Ill.: Alec R. Allenson, Inc., 1956), p. 21, cites the slurring of gutterals by Galileans as the reason for the scorn and contempt directed at them by erudite Jews from other districts: "The rabbis considered that this defective pronunciation precluded Galileans from studying the Law (T. B. Erubin 63b) and Galileans were sometimes forbidden to recite the public prayers in the synagogue (T. B. Megillah 24b)."

2. Morton S. Enslin, "New Testament Times II: Palestine," *The Interpreter's Bible* (New York: Abingdon-Cokesbury Press, 1951) vol. 7, p. 113.

3. Those desiring a fuller defense of the Pharisees against Christian charges of hypocrisy will want to consult R. Travers Herford's *Pharisees* (New York: The Macmillan Co., 1924), pp. 114–19. This work is also available as a Beacon paperback published in 1962.

4. Sota 22b (Babylonian Talmud).

5. Herford, *Pharisees,* p. 118.

6. The reader will recall mention earlier (Chapter 4) of an assassination attempt made by ten Pharisees upon the life of Herod the Great. Later, just before Herod's death in 4 B.C., Matthias and Judas met an equally grim end. Captured after inciting the Jews to tear down the figure of a gilded eagle from above the main portal of the Temple in Jerusalem, these two Pharisees were burned alive.

7. According to Ernest F. Scott, the "rise of the Synagogue may be compared, in its historical significance, with the invention of printing, though in some ways it marked an even greater revolution. By the Synagogue, God's worship was made independent of everything that was sensuous and external. He was the righteous God, and desired

that men should serve Him by moral obedience. They were to meet before Him to meditate on His will, as it was revealed in His holy law." (*The Nature of the Early Church,* New York: Chas. Scribner's Sons, 1941, pp. 71–72.)

8. Frederick C. Grant, *Roman Hellenism and the New Testament* (New York: Chas. Scribner's Sons, 1962), p. 136.

9. Herford, *Pharisees,* p. 71.

10. Morton Smith, "Palestinian Judaism in the First Century," in *Israel: Its Role in Civilization,* ed. Moshe Davis (New York: Harper and Brothers, 1956), pp. 73–74.

11. Some quotations from Louis Finkelstein's *Pharisees* (Philadelphia: The Jewish Publication Society of America, 1962–5723) indicate how ingrained some heathen superstitions were in the *'am ha-arez,* though innocently adhered to:

"No less objectionable from the sophisticated urban point of view was the continued adherence of the provincial to his ancestral superstitions. It is significant that long after the Baal worship had apparently disappeared from Israel, the field which was watered by rain was still called *Bet ha-Baal,* the territory of Baal, to distinguish it from the *Bet ha-Shelahim,* the field which was watered by irrigation. In later times, the use of this name was entirely innocent, of course, like our use of the names of pagan deities to designate the days of the week. Yet there can be no doubt that in both instances the evidence of language proves the survival of primitive thought in the minds of the people, long after they had officially been converted to the dominant religion. . . . But more important than this archaic reference to the Baal as the source of rain and fertility was the preservation of various "Amoritic" superstitions among the provincials. Among these were such practices as the carrying of bones of the dead as amulets, pouring out wine and oil on festive occasions, and especially at the reception of honored guests, and the recognition of certain days as being ill-omened" (p. 28-29).
And again:

"While the *'am-ha-arez* was pious and observant by standards other than those of Hasideans, he retained a number of rituals condemned by Prophecy and Pharisaism as virtually pagan. He would hesitate to start work on Fridays or Saturday evenings, or New Moons, preserving the Mesopotamian doctrine that the Sabbath and New Moon were days of ill-omen, but transferring the Sabbath tabu to other times. He was given to other superstitions associating relics of the dead with good or ill luck. He continued the pagan fasts and celebrations, and his defenders tried hard to find support for his views in a reconstruction of history" (pp. 758–59).

12. Ibid., pp. 26–27.

13. Ibid., p. 27.

14. Ibid., p. 97.

15. Pesahim 49b.

16. Ibid.

17. Ibid.

18. Shabbat 16.18. (Babylonian Talmud).

19. Rabbi Julian Morgenstern in *Some Significant Antecedents of Christianity* (Leiden: E. J. Brill, 1966, pp. 8–15) contends that Galilean Jews strictly conformed with the procedure established in Exodus 12: 1–14 whereby the Passover festival commenced on the eve of the fourteenth of Nisan (the first Hebrew month) with the slaying of the Paschal lamb and the eating of the meal. Jerusalemites, however, did not do this until the fifteenth of Nisan.

20. Differences in custom between Judeans and Galileans have been pointed out by reputable authorities. I have not attempted to cite every Talmudic reference, but instead direct the interested reader to p. 554 of *The Jewish Encyclopedia* (New York: Funk and Wagnalls Co., 1905); and Louis Finkelstein's *Pharisees,* pp. 46–47 (marriage), 47–48 (widows), 49–50 (funeral), 52–53 (olive purity), and 59 (fowl and milk). The difference regarding the day before the Passover (in Judea Jews worked until noon, which Galileans worked not at all on that day) is referred to in the Babylonian Talmud—Pesachim 55a.

6 But Can We Really "See" Jesus Historically?

Any drama needs more than a principal character; to appear intelligible and human, that character must be surrounded by a stage and scenery, properties and supplementary cast. Only then does the "lead role" take on personality, clarity, and meaning.

Thus we have sought to fill in more adequately than do the Gospels the historical background of Jesus. We have interrogated various factors—social, political, economic, and religious —which contributed to make Jesus the person He was. We began by reasserting the importance of Christianity's historic roots in this individual. Without questioning or demeaning the Jewish ancestry and character of Jesus, we have explored the Gentile-impregnated environment of His homeland. We have surveyed the forces and events which combined in the centuries before His birth to bring about that environment. Galilee, we discovered, was well populated, fertile, and agriculturally productive, crisscrossed by major roadways, and guarded jealously by Roman troops as part of the empire's far-eastern defense perimter. Beyond this, we have seen how extensively Greco-Roman values and attitudes infiltrated Palestinian society, beginning with the Herodian aristocracy but also filtering down to the merchant and artisan classes below. Our travels carried us farther afield through the cities of the Decapolis, which we viewed with an eye to possible implications their presence might have had for the ministry of Jesus. Finally we noted the contrast between the northern and southern Jew in custom, dialect, and mood. Palestinian Judaism was far from monolithic in its daily expression, and the cleft between the *'am ha-arez* of Galilee and zealous Pharisees is unmistakable.

Looking back, we can see now how limited and cautious our use of the Gospel records has been in corroborating our conclusions. This is understandable, for the Gospels offer scant commentary on Hellenistic influence in Galilee and, more than that, the Gospels were not designed originally as biographies in the strict, documented sense that we think of biographies today. The manner in which the Gospels open shows this: Mark introduces a stark declarative statement steeped in theological bias, "The beginning of the gospel of Jesus Christ, the Son of God"; Matthew launches into a lengthy genealogy structured to prove that Jesus was the lawful Messiah of the Jews; and Luke affirms that he is writing "an orderly account" that his reader may know the *truth* concerning those things he has been taught (1:3–4). These are not statements of impartial biographers but of convinced believers, and the same must be said of John's Gospel as well. This is to concede freely that the Gospels are as theologically slanted as the Pauline letters and equally reflect the struggles, hopes, and advanced Christology of churches in a later period.

Such an admission should not shock or offend the conscientious Christian. Though the historic fact of Jesus is important, still—from the Christian viewpoint—salvation has never hinged upon whether or not the lineaments of Jesus' activity and teaching can be wholly recovered or reconstructed. "Fortunately," to quote Dr. Grant once more, "neither the first-century Church nor the ecumenical church in any age since has ever assumed that our salvation depends upon the historicity of every detail in the Gospels." Observing that the "books of the

New Testament are all written 'out of faith' and 'to faith,' or 'through faith for faith' (cf. Rom. 1:17)," he then adds that the Christian faith "begins, not with a chapter or a volume of modern scientific biography, but with the revelation of God in Christ, the manifestation of his power, his wisdom, his goodness and love in the Man whom he has 'appointed' to judge the living and the dead; 'and of this he has given assurance to all men by raising him from the dead' (Acts 17:32)." [1]

Once we accept this faith-perspective in the Gospel, we are willing to cease imposing unrealistic expectations upon them and allow them to witness on their own terms. The Gospels are a fabric of stories, sayings, and prayers, some versions of which are more primitive than others. Before being written down over a generation after the Cross, such fragments of memorabilia were passed along by word of mouth in various localities by different teachers as normative for Christian instruction and conduct. Although some sayings of Jesus were preserved almost verbatim (Mark 8:14–21 and Luke 7:22 are candidates for such a distinction), much we possess is but a meager summary of what Jesus actually taught. This loss in transmission was natural. The ordeal of continually retelling these traditions and the variation of interest with which separate teachings were received in different areas took their toll. No attempt was made to publish an historically accurate "life" of the Nazarene: no need existed for it, since He was to return so soon in glory. Awesome, ecstatic years these were for the Church, what with God performing daily His mighty works, signs, and wonders through the Apostles as He formerly had through their Lord.

During this period of flowering faith, however, momentous changes were afoot. The center of gravity shifted in the Church from rural Palestine to urban Antioch and Rome, from Jew to Gentile. The delay in Christ's return required the Church to adjust its theology and organization. In place of simply waiting, its leaders had to act to meet rising demands for instruction of converts, aid to the destitute, and arbitration of business and family disputes. Thus it was that finally the dominant posture of the Church toward the future sufficiently weakened to allow a gaze backward which contained both a vision of its exalted and coming Lord and a curiosity regarding the earthly Jesus who went about doing good only to be "crucified and killed by the hands of lawless men" (Acts 2:23). By this time, though, it was no longer easy to fit the pieces together, as Vincent Taylor relates:

> When the time came to coordinate the original facts, the evangelists could do no more than supply the local traditions of the churches for which they wrote, traditions which vary in value and cannot in all points be reconciled. Some of the stories contain legendary details, as for example, when the risen Christ is said to have eaten a piece of broiled fish (Luke 24:42). Others are products of conscious art, as in the story of the journey to Emmaus (Luke 24:13–35), and the Johannine stories of Mary Magdalene in the garden (John 21:11–18), of Thomas (John 20:19–29), and the appearance by the Sea of Tiberias (John 21:1–14). The Marcan story of the visit of the women to the tomb (Mark 16:1–8) is a story told at Rome at a time when interest in the empty tomb had awakened." [2]

A literalistic use of the Gospels, as if a diary of Jesus, is thus soon doomed to frustration. Accepted on their own ground, the Gospels are the product of an evangelistic desire to offer in durable and teachable form the saving proclamation of what God had done in Jesus Christ, what even at that moment of writing He was doing, and what He would continue to do as the present evil age ground to an end and the new age of righteousness and peace dawned. Incidents in the life of Jesus are therefore set in accordance with certain evangelical interests. In this, Mark led off and the other Gospel writers followed. Mark, for instance, wanted to stress the irresistible appeal of Jesus which led His disciples to abandon at once their families and businesses without a second thought. An artificiality clings, therefore, to the call of the disciples (1:16–20; 2:14), as though Jesus were a total stranger to Simon and Andrew, James and John, and Levi.

Mark is also overly anxious to center his reader's attention upon the crucifixion drama in Jerusalem and to fix the blame for that injustice upon the Jews. He consequently jumps the gun on reality by making the Pharisees appear so hostile toward Jesus *from the first* that they immediately join forces with the Herodians, whose Roman ways and fashion the Pharisees normally spurned. Of course a common threat can turn enemies into bedfellows, but not that painlessly.

The implications of all this are enough to make any student of the New Testament hesitate. If the Gospel writers, to start with, were selective in what they preserved regarding the historical Jesus; if then the fragments of tradition they chose were presented so as to be in agreement with certain theological assumptions held later in churches; if, on top of this, justification of later Christian practices and prejudices swayed the recounting of episodes—then it must be asked if the Gospels have any value for the person who wishes to "see" Jesus historically.

Before despairing, though, we must remember that factors in the Church operated from earliest times to control teaching and combat heresy. For one thing, the Redeemer was no phantom. Unlike the heroes of heathen mystery religions, the Nazarene had labored, taught, traveled, bled, and died like any other human being. This alone tended to curb religious fantasy. The presence of eyewitnesses posed another reason. Members of the mother Church in Jerusalem had personally heard Jesus teach; some of them undoubtedly had received private instruction from Him. This would be equally true of some Christians who lived on in Galilee after the Resurrection. Not to be overlooked were also the enemies of Jesus and later of the Church; among them were eyewitnesses, and how readily they would have fastened upon any distortions of fact in order to discredit Christian missionaries.

It thus becomes my position that while many details about Jesus have been lost in transmission, sufficient material survives to give glimpses of His person and echoes of His voice. How remarkable it is that stories and teachings circulating years after in urban centers like Antioch, Alexandria, Ephesus, and Rome should retain much of their original rural and open-air flavor! The beauty of Galilee, the energy of its people is felt in references to fishermen sorting their catch, women grinding meal, children playing, sons rebelling, birds flying, flowers blooming, grass burning in ovens, houses washing away in a cloudburst, sheep wandering off, patches tearing away from unshrunk cloth, seed falling on heartless soil. The topics discussed reflect Galilee (fasting, ritual purity, sabbath observance, Roman taxes, fraternization with "sinners") as opposed to those which monopolized the attention of later Christians (circumcision and the mission to Gentiles, speaking in tongues and the Holy Spirit, baptism and the unity of the Church, Resurrection and the Lord's return).

As for details regarding Jesus Himself, the most irrefutable, of course, concern His death. Christian sources emphatically agree that during the procuratorship of Pontius Pilate in Judea, the Roman authorities crucified Jesus, presumably as an insurrectionist.

Beyond these facts, however, certainty quickly falters, and we are left to draw such deductions as we can, based upon logical assumptions. Drawn from the investigations of Ernst Lohmeyer,[3] one assumption is that the "Son of Man" passages are primitive, Galilean, and close to the human Jesus. Günther Bornkamm seconds this conclusion, although cautiously, saying that *some* of the "Son of Man" references can be traced back without doubt to Jesus, among them those instances where the disciples are addressed directly, such as, "And I tell you, everyone who acknowledges me before men, the Son of man also will acknowledge before the angels of God; but he who denies me before men will be denied before the angels of God" (Luke 12:8–9; Mark 8:38). This reference to Jesus in the third person which links the Final Judgment with men's acceptance or rejection of Jesus,

Bornkamm views as the place "where we come up against the original core of the tradition, Jesus' own words." [4]

A second assumption is that pro-poverty and anti-wealth references spring from more primitive traditions. Lohmeyer has detected in early Galilean Christanity a requirement of poverty based upon the belief that somehow "the poor" per se are more acceptable and pleasing to God than the rich. As stated already, Jesus grew to manhood amid the *'am ha-arez,* many of whom lived submarginal lives due to oppressive taxes and the vicissitudes of nature. The message of Jesus undoubtedly first took root in this working class. Hence His commandment to "go, sell what you have, and give to the poor" takes on added authenticity as does His teaching, "How hard it will be for those who have riches to enter the kingdom of God!" (Mark 10:21, 23)

Sherman E. Johnson has raised yet a third clue or assumption. He submits that a mark of earliest tradition "may be the presence of ideas and situations which more naturally belong to the Galilean environment than to Judea or regions outside Palestine." [5] Applying this principle, he believes the following passages to be unquestionably Palestinian and "as close as possible to the story of Jesus himself": the Sabbath controversy (Mark 2:23–28), the denunciation of Pharisees (Luke 11:14–12:12), and the healing of a paralytic (Mark 2:1–12). Other controversies seen as quite possibly derived from Galilean tradition, although with less positive evidence, are the heated exchanges over ceremonial purity (Matt. 23:25–39, Luke 11:39), Jesus' eating with tax collectors and sinners (Mark 2:15–17), and the charge of his being in league with a Syrian deity, Beelzebul (Matt. 12:22–32; Mark 3:22–30; Luke 11:14–23).

A fourth assumption is that material embarrassing or undesirable in early Church circles may be ruled authentic. In this category falls the slanderous gossip implied in the retort of Jesus, "The Son of man came eating and drinking, and they say, 'Behold, a glutton and a drunkard'" (Matt. 11:16; Luke 7:31–

34), and His belief that not only would tax collectors but prosti-
tutes enter the kingdom of God before His critics (Matt. 21:31).
If women as well as men became His disciples, as is likely, what
more convenient slur could His enemies spread abroad than that
Jesus was morally loose?

Also unwelcome in the early Church was the rejection by
Jesus of certain practices advocated by John the Baptist. The
"eating and drinking" statement just cited reveals His renuncia-
tion of John's asceticism. One can feel the Jerusalem Church
squirm at teachings of Jesus which diminished the importance of
fasting, but which were too well remembered to be denied. The
best that could be done in the case of Mark 2:18–22 (Matt.
9:14–17; Luke 5:33–38) was to dilute the unwanted repudia-
tion of fasting (Mark 2:21–22) by prefacing it with an acceptable Church explanation inserted into the mouth of Jesus: "Can
the children of the bridechamber fast while the bridegroom is
with them?" (Mark 2:19–20). The same scurry to dilute the
effect of an undesirable but undeniable difference between Jesus
and the Baptist is sensed in the Fourth Gospel, where a later
boast of the Church that Jesus baptized more disciples than
John is inserted ahead of the unwanted statement that Jesus in
reality baptized none but His disciples (John 4:1–2).

It can be said with reasonable certainty, therefore, that Palestinian Christian communities were disturbed by such divergent
fragments of memory. The Baptist's following was numerous
and vocal long after the Resurrection;[6] indeed, for some decades it was a lively rival to Christianity. Had the Church—especially the early Jerusalem fellowship—been able to erase from
living tradition any allusion to disagreement between Jesus and
the Baptist, the Church would have gladly done so for the sake
of attracting more of John's following to its ranks.

Finally, in summary fashion, we should note the long-standing but still valuable discussion by P. W. Schmiedel in the *Encyclopaedia Biblica*.[7] His premise is that credible passages concerning Jesus are recognizable in the synoptic Gospels (Mat-

thew, Mark, and Luke), and that these passages—nine in number—form "the foundation-pillars for a truly scientific life of Jesus." He writes that when a secular historian "finds before him a historical document which testifies to the worship of a hero unknown to other sources, he attaches first and foremost importance to those features which cannot be deduced merely from the fact of this worship, and he does so on the simple and sufficient ground that they would not be found in this source unless the author had met with them as fixed data of tradition." [8] Convinced that the "same fundamental principle may safely be applied in the case of the gospels" because all of them were written by worshippers of Jesus, Schmiedel then offers supportive arguments in behalf of the "pillar passages" below.

And Jesus said to him, "Why do you call me good? No one is good but God alone. You know the commandments: . . . You lack one thing; go sell what you have, and give to the poor, and you will have treasure in heaven; and come, follow me." (Mark 10:18–21)

I tell you, every sin and blasphemy will be forgiven men, but the blasphemy against the Spirit will not be forgiven. (Matt. 12:31)

And when his friends heard it, they went out to seize him, for they said, "He is beside himself." (Mark 3:21)

But of that day or that hour no one knows, not even the angels in heaven, nor the Son, but only the Father. (Mark 13:32)

"Eloi, Eloi, lama sabachthani?" which means: "My God, my God, why hast thou forsaken me?" (From the Cross as recorded by Mark 15:34; Matt. 27:46)

And he cautioned them, saying, "Take heed, beware of the leaven of the Pharisees and the leaven of Herod." And they discussed it with one another, saying, "We have no bread." And being aware of it, Jesus said to them, "Why do you discuss the fact that you have no bread? Do you not yet perceive or understand? Are your hearts hardened?" (Mark 8:14–21)

The blind receive their sight and the lame walk, lepers are cleansed and the deaf hear, and the dead are raised up, and the poor have good news preached to them. (The message sent by Jesus to John the Baptist as recorded in Matt. 11:5; Luke 7:22)

Why does this generation seek a sign? Truly, I say to you, no sign shall be given to this generation. (Mark 8:12; Matt. 12:39, 16:4; Luke 11:29)

And he could do no mighty work there [Nazareth], except that he laid his hands upon a few sick people and healed them. And he marveled because of their disbelief. (Mark 6:5–6)

Schmiedel draws three deductions from these "pillar" references. Concerning the devotion exhibited toward Jesus, he states that even the thoroughly disinterested historian must recognize his duty to investigate "this great reverence for himself which Jesus was able to call forth; and he will then, first and foremost, find himself led to recognize as true the two great facts that Jesus had compassion for the multitudes and that he preached with power, not as the scribes" (Matt. 9:36, 7:29).[9] Another deduction relates to the necessary ingredient of faith. According to Mark 6:5, says Schmiedel, "we are to understand that Jesus healed where he found faith. This power is so strongly attested throughout the first and second centuries that, in view of the spiritual greatness of Jesus and the imposing character of his personality, it would be indeed difficult to deny it to him."[10] A third and final deduction concerns the purely religious-ethical utterances of Jesus in relation to which Schmiedel feels "we are most advantageously placed."[11] Here especially he thinks a maxim laid down earlier applies, namely, that everything which "harmonizes with the idea of Jesus" as derived from the pillar passages and "is not otherwise open to fatal objection" may be accepted as credible. This conclusion, while bold, reflects neither recklessness nor naïveté. Schmiedel acknowledges that the ethical teachings of Jesus show traces of being "unconsciously modified in accord with conditions of the Christian community

that arose at a later date"; he concedes that "they may have un-
dergone some distortion of their meaning through transference
to a connection that does not belong to them." Nevertheless, this
cautious scholar adds, "the spirit which speaks in them is quite
unmistakable."

With this we close our exploration of Gospel credibility, particularly that of the three synoptics. It is a question some have
felt irrelevant, others irreverent, but which is unavoidable in fair-
ness to what follows.

NOTES

1. Frederick C. Grant, *An Introduction to New Testament Thought*
New York: Abingdon Press, 1950), p. 50.

2. Vincent Taylor, "The Life and Ministry of Jesus," *The Interpreter's Bible*, vol. 7 p. 144.

3. Ernst Lohmeyer, *Galiläa und Jerusalem* (Göttingen: Vandenhoeck
and Ruprecht, 1936).

4. Günther Bornkamm, *Jesus of Nazareth* (New York: Harper and
Brothers, 1960), p. 176.

5. Sherman E. Johnson, "Jesus and First-Century Galilee," in
Schmauch, *Memoriam Ernst Lohmeyer*, pp. 77–78.

6. In addition to the testimony of Josephus (*Antiquities* xviii. 5, 2)
concerning the wide influence of John the Baptist, we find mention
in Acts (18:24–19:7) of Christian missionaries converting disciples
of John in Ephesus; and in the first half of the third century the
Christian apologist, Origin, asserting that Jews did not consider John
the Baptist a Christian (*Celsus* i. 41)

7. See the "Gospels" section of the *Encyclopaedia Biblica* II, columns
1872–89.

8. Ibid., col. 1872.

9. Ibid., cols. 1872–73.

10. Ibid., col. 1884.

11. Ibid., col. 1889.

7 The Lull before the Storm

And he said to them, "How is it that you sought me? Did you not know I must be in my Father's house?"

—Luke 2:49

And he went down with them and came to Nazareth, and was obedient to them. . . . And Jesus grew in wisdom and stature and in favor with God and men.

—Luke 2:51–52

That the Gospels are more theological than biographical can at once be seen in their almost total silence regarding the childhood and adolescence of Jesus. Only Luke breaks the silence with his account of the first visit to the Temple. This silence, however, is not unusual. Ancient writers commonly ignored the juvenile years of their heroes in order to concentrate attention upon adult exploits. The Hebrew Scriptures themselves say nothing of the early years of the prophet Elijah, and refer only to the birth and adoption of Moses (Exod. 2:1–10).

Obviously the exception in Luke is deliberate. At a much later date the opinion grew in Christian circles that the inspiration and spiritual uniqueness of Jesus was evident earlier than at His baptism by John. This view promoted the tradition of the first Temple visit as we have it now (Luke 2:41–51), a story based perhaps upon a kernel of truth but embellished by Christian zeal, polished by the Evangelist, and presented as proof that the child Jesus already enjoyed a unique relationship to God. To this tradition Luke adds for emphasis the observation that Jesus increased in wisdom and stature and in favor with God and man (2:40; 2:51). Having shown the youthful Jesus to be independent of spirit, Luke pictures Him as no less obedient to His parents. Together the three return to Nazareth, a community in lower Galilee that the Gospels agree was His home town.

There Jesus, shaped by influences of differing character and intensity, grew to manhood. No more is heard of Joseph, the father. Presumably he died before Jesus reached maturity, leaving a widow with five sons and at least two daughters. Jesus, as the eldest son, became head of the family. He continued in the building trade that He had been taught until He was moved to travel and teach. When that break from Nazareth and family ties came is uncertain, but tradition places it about the age of thirty. Why Jesus waited so long is also unclear. Perhaps the needs of a widowed mother with minor children held Him at home until finally the preaching of John the Baptist overrode family obligations.

Nazareth, as Jesus knew it, appears to have covered a greater area than it does now. Excavations there reveal that the first-century community stretched more than a hundred yards farther along the adjoining slope so as to include more than sixty caves, some having several levels and connecting passages forming underground refuges useful in periods of armed conflict. Enclosing the plateau on which the town is situated, hills rise to form an amphitheater broken only on the southeast by a wadi. In Jesus' day the slopes had not as yet been denuded of trees by passing armies, and sufficient soil remained to make farming possible. Ranging outward from the dwellings, therefore, were fig and olive groves, barley fields and vineyards—a panoply of fruits and crops to be carefully tended and brought to harvest. While some villagers labored in the open, others at home made clothing, sandals, tent cloth, furniture, and saddles for personal use or sale. After this fashion Jesus undoubtedly worked at home on donkey litters, wooden plows, yokes, lampstands, chairs, and tables. Out of doors He would have built houses and walls, wine and olive presses, grain silos and cisterns. Most of the houses constructed of sun-hardened brick or tamped earth were crude by current standards, but some in the area were of limestone, so that Jesus was in all likelihood a mason as well as a carpenter.

The years at Nazareth were thus full and anything but silent. They overflowed with the sights, sounds, and activities that mark many a Gospel parable. T. R. Glover describes Nazareth as an Oriental town "with poor houses, bad smells and worse stories, tragedies of widow and prodigal son, of unjust judge and grasping publican." [1] So much was there to teach the observant, energetic lad. At first the child could only toddle after His mother to the village spring, but soon enough He was off with playmates re-enacting some deeds of bravery by Gideon or David's men. How youthful imagination must have exerted itself amid fierce shouts and boisterous laughter!

The Synagogue also had much to teach. Listening and then reciting over and over again, Jesus learned the history and law of His people. If the Gospels are correct as to Scripture Jesus later quoted, He was most fond of passages that stressed the mercy of God and the duty to love one's fellowman. The writings of Second Isaiah, Hosea, Jeremiah, Jonah, and Ezekiel stirred Him, as did the yearnings of the Psalmist. He became acquainted with the promises held out in Daniel and possibly the visions shining in the Book of Enoch.

The marketplace and nearby roadways were teachers. As a boy on an errand, Jesus had merely to listen to laborers growling about taxes and low wages. Travelers carried word of rebels hiding arms in caves to the east. Word may well have come of Herodian quislings drowned in the lake by Zealots as a warning.[2] On His initial visit to the Temple, Jesus could hardly have missed seeing porticoes blackened by fire and being told how legionaries reacted to riots. Roman governors appointed and deposed high priests with disconcerting ease and on occasion seized sacred funds to cover up their own waste. News of such acts traveled fast and far. Thus as Jesus grew into young manhood, it mattered little that He was not privy to Roman political strategy nor invited to a Herodian banquet. Walls have ears, fields have eyes, and Jesus needed only recall stories related in Nazareth of expensive feasts and military maneuvers to grasp the scope of exploitation, slavery, and tyranny current in His time. That He met and conversed with members of the Jewish underground is highly probable.

The mood of Jesus' childhood home was thus conservative after the manner of the Galilean *'am ha-arez,* the family belonging "to the Jewish part of the population which, since the times of the Maccabees, had reattached themselves to the temple cult in Jerusalem and the legal practices of Judaism." [3] While Nazareth stood in the shadow of heavily pagan Sepphoris, it also stood but two miles northeast of Japha, a Jewish town with a synagogue at its heart. Significantly it was this thoroughly Jewish town that Josephus chose to fortify in A.D. 66 when a Roman army moved against his rebel forces.

Pursuing the same line of investigation, let it be added that nothing suggests that the Nazareth population was descended from Gentiles compelled by Maccabean swords to adopt Judaism. Jesus and other breadwinners in Nazareth admittedly spoke Greek as an economic necessity,[4] but Aramaic continued the mother tongue of Palestinian Jews. The Jewish character of Jesus' family appears in the names of His four brothers (Jacob, Joseph, Judah, and Simeon), all of them those of patriarchs. The name of Jesus originates in the Hebrew *Joshua,* more fully *Yehoshua* meaning "Yahweh is salvation." [5] Note, furthermore, that while the Gospels depict Jesus in open conflict with synagogue authorities, they nowhere infer that He was a libertine or iconoclast. Instead He continues to worship on the Sabbath and to honor synagogue teaching even when having reservations about its teachers. Temple graft and commercialism probably saddened and at times angered Jesus as it did other pilgrims from afar,[6] but nothing indicates that He rejected outright the sacrificial rites or the Temple as an institution.

We have before us, then, the portrait of a young builder growing up in a home where Jewish piety marked His formative years and drew from Him a lasting devotion to God and man. Together with His family He attended the village synagogue and made at least some pilgrimages to Jerusalem, although how regularly the Gospels leave in doubt. The Galilean *'am ha-arez* were criticized for laxity in this respect, and the family of Jesus may well have been limited by cost and distance from making the journey annually as prescribed.

Here we might leave matters concerning Jesus' boyhood and youth but for the existence of the semi-pagan atmosphere which surrounded Him. What Jesus did not learn one way He learned another, every experience—negative as well as positive—teaching Him something. Though steeped in the pietism of a Jewish family, He felt the siren influence of a wider pagan world. The often fanatical patriotism of Galileans was due to strong heathen counter-currents. After the example of Ezra (10:11), the object of much in Judaism was to separate its followers from Gentiles and keep them faithful to their Covenant agreement, but in the achievement of this Judaism was not wholly successful even among the lower classes in Palestine. Martin P. Nilsson asserts that

> In the Hellenistic age the peoples were not separated by water-tight compartments, not even the Jews in spite of their pride in their Law and customs and their contempt for and even hatred against other peoples. The lower classes were, although they adhered to the Law and the Pharisees, accessible to ideas of love and equity which appealed to them. For the people are never consistent in their thinking. The great difficulty, which may be an impossibility, is to know which of the ideas current in the Hellenistic age penetrated the people and got

hold of them under the surface of the prevailing legalism and nationalism. And Jesus spoke to the people.

My last suppositions may be rejected and they are but suppositions. But it is certain that the Jewish people was surrounded by Hellenistic influences, not only in the diaspora but also in its own country, and this fact should be taken duly into account. . . . Certainly the Jews were opposed to the Hellenistic tendencies, and this opposition was strengthened by the attempt to impose Hellenism by force. One learns something even from adversaries and gets impetus from them and this is probably true of the Jews also. It is probably true of the lower classes too, which did not reflect on their beliefs and customs but unthinkingly embraced the ideas which they heard and which appealed to them.[7]

In view of this, the saying attributed to Jesus, "Go nowhere among the Gentiles" (Matt. 10:5) becomes untintelligible. It must be ruled a later church prohibition placed in His mouth, Jesus needing to go nowhere to be among Gentiles because Gentiles and their way of life were all about Him. Galilee was "the meeting ground of Hellenism, the Jewish revolutionary spirit, and . . . Pharisiaism," [8] and we can be sure Jesus frequently felt the collision of these irreconcilable forces. To begin with, probably much of our discussion of the *'am ha-arez* applies to Him. Galilean Jews, though loyal to the Torah, were loyal in their own way, clinging to fundamental precepts and leaving the fine points to scholars. While allegiance to the Yahweh cult had not completely disappeared in Galilee due to earlier enemy invasions and colonization, the area had been Judaized only a century before Jesus. Hence to a large degree it retained the character of the Diaspora or heathen lands to which Jews had been deported. Relatively untouched by the strict doctrinal and scholastic training centered in Jerusalem, Galilee was thus open to non-Jewish ideas and movements from abroad. For this reason Galilean Jews before the fall of Jerusalem were less Pharisaic than is commonly supposed. As we have seen, they often set an independent course, and, although the deviations are not fully discernible, sufficient evidence is present to indicate that Jesus belonged to an unofficial strain of Judaism which reflected extensive exposure to foreign influence.

More than thirty years ago the scholar Rudolph Otto documented the existence of such an "unofficial Judaism." Dr. Otto declares Jesus to be "one of a class" which rabbis of that period refer to as " *'ober gelila'ah'* (Galilean itinerant). In particular He was an itinerant preacher of eschatology." [9]

We should pause to record here that Hebrew and Jewish writings, with few exceptions, assume that the whole of human history exists under the judgment of God. Far from being a meaningless series of cycles as pagans saw it, history was moving purposefully toward the accomplishment of God's will. In the end God would triumph, evil would be vanquished, and oppressors would be punished. The man of faith had but to look deep enough, like the prophet Habbakkuk, to see that "still the vision awaits its time; it hastens to the end—it will not lie" (Hab. 2:3).

Rudolph Otto thus is right in saying that "Jesus' message of the kingdom did not fall from the skies as a complete novelty, but had long been prepared for. In particular, Jesus' preaching of the kingdom is manifestly connected with . . . an earlier historical phenomenon, i.e. the later Jewish eschatology and apocalyptic." [10] This later apocalyptic strain in Jewish literature is characterized by a kind of firebrand prophecy not easily accepted in staid rabbinical circles.[11] The drama of conflict and redemption is not seen as political or historical, but as supernatural, cosmic, angelic. Dependence on human effort and insight is abandoned in favor of utter reliance upon divine or heavenly resources. Most of all, the mood of the apocalyptic is that of extreme tension arising from persecution, pessimism, and uncertainty as to the future. When people are convinced that life has become about as dark and desperate as it can get, they most naturally embrace such a view.

This apocalypticism, however, was not, according to Rudolph

Otto, purely Jewish "if one understands by that term something which derived and developed from purely Israelite traditions. Rather, being a late Jewish form, it was inherited from ancient Judaism, but with an intrusive element which came not from that source but from the Chaldean and Iranian east." [12]

How did this intrusion come about, we ask. Rudolph Otto explains:

> As far as Israel was concerned, there is no doubt that the occasion when eastern influences of this sort made themselves felt was the captivity in Babylonia (and Media) a region where Persian and Chaldean ideas mingled. In detail, the eschatological systems such as were put together in the apocalyptic book of Enoch, and on which the eschatology of Jesus and his circle was largely dependent and modelled, 'point to North Palestine' (C. Beer) as their place of origin. Galilee was a land through which pilgrims journeyed on their way from the eastern Jewish diaspora in Babylonia. At the same time, Galilee was closely connected with Syria by highways and foreign residents, and by a Jewish diaspora which had spread out from Galilee as far as Tyre, Sidon, Damascus, and through Syria generally.[13]

The argument then moves on to an emphatic conclusion.

> In any case, late Jewish eschatology was not purely Jewish. Likewise the strict differentiation usually made between Palestinian, Oriental, and Hellenistic is open to question. Even Jesus' eschatology of the kingdom of God was not purely Palestinian. The apocalyptic teaching which has come to us from him had long contained elements which did not originate in Palestine. And to make 'Palestinian' a test of whether a certain word was or was not actually spoken by Jesus is a mistake from the start, because 'Palestinian' is itself an uncertain norm. Not even 'Gnostic' is a reliable canon of spuriousness. For as Gressmann correctly says (*Zeitschrift für Kirchengeschichte*, 1922, p. 179): "Gnosis is of the very spirit of apocalyptic teaching. And even as early as Enoch's apocalypticism, on which Jesus was dependent, we find definite

gnostic traits and terms. . . . Official Judaism turned away from Hellenistic religion and became a rigid legal religion, which found its final form in the Talmud. Another stream, which one can designate unofficial Judaism, led in a straight line to Jesus." [14]

Not everyone will wish to follow out to its destination this train of argument that Jesus, as a Galilean, belonged to an unofficial Judaism that was not typically Jewish. Some will wish to get off at one station or another along the way. Indeed, some will wish to avoid boarding the train at all. The final conclusion nevertheless appears to have substance, the question being only to what degree foreign concepts and ideas became implanted in the Jewish masses in Palestine.

Where in this picture, of course, the "Son of Man" material fits is not easily determined. As stated before, some of those references may be traceable to Jesus, though current scholarships is hard pressed to agree whether or not Jesus actually used the term "Son of Man," and what it meant to Him if He did. Again the question forces itself upon us: How much of this material in the synoptic Gospels originates with Jesus, and how much with the Church, which, prior to the writing of the synoptics, underwent several decades of intense religious excitement? The figure of the "Son of Man," which for Jesus may have meant a supernatural agent coming upon the clouds of Heaven, soon came in Christian thinking to refer to the risen Jesus expected momentarily to return.[15] Hence one must feel his way. Günther Bornkamm, among others, reveals this. In the "synoptic apocalypse" (Mark 13), he sees the direction of Jesus' message as probably being "Take heed, watch" (13:33), but beyond this he proceeds cautiously. He concludes that the Gospel material originated in late Jewish apocalypticism, and was taken over in oral transmission as sayings of Jesus which refer to "war and rebellions, earthquakes and famines, darkness and falling stars, the laying waste of Judaea and the desecration of the temple." Other sayings attributed to Jesus in Mark 13 reflect the later experiences of the

Church, such as persecution and the rise of false doctrines. There is the possibility, however, that interwoven in this material are genuine sayings of Jesus.[16]

Our view of the Nazareth years is consequently blurred at many points; where we could wish to see face to face, we must be content to see only as "in a mirror dimly." Still, the outline of a historic personage begins to take shape. His childhood and adolescent years can be sketched with some confidence.

It also becomes clear that Nazareth at best was enclosed by a largely pagan environment where hatred and suspicion, racial and religious taboos hampered social relations. Equally apparent is the fact that, despite its productivity, Galilee was a conquered land, the mass of its Jewish inhabitants burdened heart, hand, and soul by economic and political oppression. They yearned for the release promised with the coming of the Messiah who would usher in the "day of consolation," reestablish the throne of David, and set wrongs right. While many simply prayed, others—bands of guerrillas—took to the sword in periodic attempts to force the hand of divine retribution through insurrection. The conviction was growing that the sands of injustice had nearly run out, that surely the righteous God of Israel must soon unleash His fury in behalf of a people long subjugated. Let any native leader appear, and a shiver of excitation rippled through the *'am ha-arez* of Palestine, bringing about him those wandering and discontent, devout and hopeful, curious and enquiring. John the Baptist was such a leader, and Jesus therefore went to the Jordan to identify Himself with John's call to repentance. Already the ax was sweeping downward at the root of the tree; any tree bearing evil fruit would be cut down and burned.[17]

The association with John, however, was but temporary. Before long Jesus was off attracting a following of His own. He might have returned to Nazareth, but that hill town was no longer suitable for the kind of summons Jesus desired to issue. Capernaum was the place to start, and there He made His home where a major road passed and eager fishing folk provided ready listeners. The *'am ha-arez* synagogue in Nazareth supplied a foundation, but Jesus was neither encased nor insulated by the teachings He received there. Long before He called out, "He who has ears to hear, let him hear!" [18] Jesus had been aware of a larger world waiting for reconciliation and healing. To read the Gospels with feeling is to sense behind them One who listened and watched, pondered and planned with a real depth of spiritual sensitivity.

What followed was natural. The first disciples, recruited from among rugged Galilean fishermen, displayed an inquisitive, aggressive spirit despite their obvious faults. Jesus appealed to the larger experience and broader ways of thought found in Galilee, and the Galileans heard Him gladly. Soon His teaching and healing attracted an audience from beyond the Jordan, from Tyre and Sidon and Judea. Like other charismatic figures, Jesus radiated a certain indefinable and yet undeniable magnetism. His imaginative teaching left inquirers fascinated and pensive, some alienated, but few indifferent. Galilee was ripe for the message of Jesus, and His voice was heard, His spirit caught. This was the world of Jesus' most impressionable and formative years, and amid such an atmosphere He taught and healed, went into hiding and came out boldly.

J. B. Phillips states that the physical and geographical background of Jesus' life has no special importance. "The setting," he says, "is in a sense 'accidental.' It happened in Palestine two thousand years ago, but it might just as well have been India, or South Africa, or Germany, or China." [19] That is doubtful. Granted that the setting in Galilee is accidental, it is not unimportant. One questions whether such a vital life, creative mind, venturesome spirit as that seen in the Gospels could have arisen anywhere else but where it did, in first-century Palestine. Putting the issue another way, we might ask: Given the fact that lower Judea was more "traditional, orthodox and secure," what would have been the natural consequence had Jesus grown to manhood in Bethlehem rather than in Nazareth? What conceivably might have ensued had He made Jerusalem his base of operations rather than Capernaum? Under such circumstances, would any religious movement following in His wake have been as missionary or inclusive as later turned out to be the case? Would there have been a Crucifixion, much less a Resurrection experience? Would Christianity have succeeded in shedding the swaddling clothes of Palestinian Judaism? Or would it have become but another Jewish sect?

These questions, of course, are unanswerable in any absolute fashion, but they set one to wondering. And with this we turn to the Capernaum phase of Jesus' life.

NOTES

1. T. R. Glover, *The Jesus of History* (New York, Harper and Brother, 1916), p. 36.

2. What Josephus describes as happening during the reign of Herod the Great (*Antiquities* XIV. xv, 10; *War* I. xvii, 2) was likely to have been repeated later.

3. Günther Bornkamm, *Jesus of Nazareth* (New York, Harper and Brothers, 1960), p. 53.

4. The debate over what language or languages Jesus spoke has continued a long time. Strong advocates have supported any one of three candidates—Hebrew, Aramaic, and Greek. Taking each in turn, one finds that in the past the use of Hebrew has been severely questioned. P. W. Schmiedel, in *Encyclopaedia Biblica* col. 1871, (New York: The Macmillan Co., 1903), states that the "masses did not understand Hebrew," and Rabbi Joseph Klausner on page 235 of *Jesus of Nazareth* (New York: The Macmillan Co., 1949) suspects that Jesus possibly "only heard the Law read in Hebrew and translated into Aramaic, his spoken language." Of late, though, the wind has shifted. Harris Birkeland argues in *The Language of Jesus* (Oslo: I kommisjon hos J. Dybwad, 1954) that Jesus normally used a colloquial dialect of Hebrew and only occasionally spoke Aramaic. M. Black in his article, "The Recovery of the Language of Jesus" (*New Testament Studies* 15, July, 1958, pp. 183–97) favors Aramaic but allows that Jesus might also have used Hebrew "on such solemn occasions . . . as at the

Institution of the Lord's Supper." Black concedes, however, that he has not seen J. M. Grintz's article, "Hebrew as the Spoken and Written Language in the Last Days of the Second Temple" (*Journal of Biblical Literature* 79, 1960, pp. 32–47) in which Mishnaic Hebrew rather than Aramaic is declared the popular language of Palestine.

As for Aramaic, its use by Jesus has been widely accepted. This language, while less highly developed than Greek, was the vernacular of the Persian Empire that the army of Alexander the Great conquered. Still firmly fastened upon first-century Palestine, Aramaic was therefore the most natural tongue of the Galilean *'am ha-arez*. This naturalness displays itself in Mark's Gospel in Aramaic sayings attributed to Jesus: "Talitha cumi" and "Ephphatha" and "Abba" (5:41, 7:34, and 14:36 respectively). It should also be noted that the familiar "My God, my God, why hast thou forsaken me?" is quoted from Psalm 22 in Aramaic. The natural use of this Semitic tongue is reflected in puns or plays upon words which are lost in Matthew 10:30 and 23:24 save as expressed in Aramaic (Bruce M. Metzger in *The Interpreter's Bible*, vol. 7, p. 53).

In contrast to the general acceptance of Aramaic as spoken by Jesus, we find Greek hard beset until recently by detractors like Maurice Goguel: "It is very doubtful whether he [Jesus] ever knew Greek. There were, it is true, a good many people in Galilee who spoke Greek; but they were mostly minor officials and shopkeepers as well as the inhabitants of the larger towns like Tiberias or Sepphoris; but Jesus did not frequent such places" (*Jesus and the Origins of Christianity*, vol. 2, New York: Harper Torchbooks, 1960, p. 261). Now, however, koine Greek has been recognized as used widely throughout all classes of Palestinian Jews. I shall not attempt to include here every supporting argument for this, but shall refer those wishing a fuller treatment of the subject to the following articles: G. H. Thompson's "To What Extent Did Jesus Use Greek?," *Religion in Life* 32 (Winter, 1962–63), pp. 103–15; and Robert H. Gundry's "The Language Milieu of First-Century Palestine," *Journal of Biblical Literature* 83, part IV (Dec., 1964), pp. 404–08.

There is no reason to feel, therefore, that Jesus could not (or would not) speak Greek sufficiently to meet the requirements of His building trade. Speaking Greek did not make Him a Philhellene or Hellenist; indeed He, unlike Paul the Apostle (Acts 17:28), displays no knowledge of Greek poetry and philosophy. In all probability Jesus did what most others did: He alternated between Greek and Aramaic depending upon who the other party was. As L. E. Elliott-Binns summarily states, "Even if intercourse with Greek towns and their Gentile inhabitants was avoided for patriotic reasons, a knowledge of Greek, even if superficial, would be so useful that the opportunity of acquiring it must have been seized by many. [Dalman] suggests . . . that the careless pronunciation of Aramaic by the Galileans may have been due to the widespread use of Greek" (*Galilean Christianity,* pp. 21–22).

5. *Yahweh* is the revered Hebrew name for God as interpreted by Moses at Sinai. It was *Yahweh,* and none other, who liberated the Israelites from slavery, guided them through the wilderness and established them as a nation in Canaan. "To worship Yahweh," writes Bernhard Anderson, "was to remember that revealing event, to accept its demand, and to live in its promise" (*Understanding the Old Testament,* Englewood Cliffs, N.J.: Prentice-Hall, 1966, p. 42).

6. During the half-century preceding the razing of the Temple in A.D. 70, a feeling of disenchantment appears to have developed among Jews who arrived as pilgrims from abroad. These "Hellenists" spoke Greek fluently, having been born and reared in foreign lands; and they were acquainted with Hellenistic culture and thus possessed a world view and freedom of thought not present in many Jews living in the Jerusalem area. (One is reminded of the disillusionment of a young German monk, Martin Luther, after he first visited Rome as a pilgrim.) By the time of Jerusalem's destruction, discontent had also appeared in the lower priesthood, the high priests having become so unpopular that the lower orders of priests turned against them, though for reasons not altogether clear. S. G. F. Brandon in his *Jesus and the Zealots* (New York: Scribner's, 1968, pp. 113–14) declares that so bitter did the antagonism become that the lower clergy finally joined forces with the Zealots, whereupon the high priests retaliated by cutting off the lower priests' Temple tithes. Now obviously the disillusionment and strife described here belong to a period thirty to forty years after Jesus, but the cancer of suspicion and discontent was probably already present during his lifetime, and slowly mounting.

7. Martin P. Nilsson, *The Historical Hellenistic Background of the New Testament* (Cambridge, Mass.: Harvard University Press, 1941), pp. 30–31.

8. Sherman E. Johnson, "Jesus and First-Century Galilee" in Schmauch, *Memoriam Ernst Lohmeyer,* p. 76.

9. Rudolph Otto, *The Kingdom of God and the Son of Man* (London: Lutterworth Press, 1938), p. 13.

10. Ibid., p. 14.

11. M. S. Enslin affirms that one of "the most conspicuous characteristics of the rabbinical literature—Mishnah, Talmuds, and Midrashes— is their silence about all that can be styled 'apocalyptic.' Thus it is easy to dismiss apocalypticism from normative Judaism, and it has been not infrequently done. It is true so far as educated, literary Judaism is concerned. They studiedly ignored this wildfire literature" (*The Prophet from Nazareth,* p. 107).

12. Otto, *Kingdom of God,* p. 14.

13. Ibid., p. 14–15.

14. Ibid., p. '15.

15. Two references mirror particularly the apocalyptic fervor in the Early Church: Mark 14:62 and Acts 7:56.

16. Bornkamm, *Jesus of Nazareth,* p. 93.

17. Matt. 3:10 and Luke 3:9; Matt. 7:16–20 and Luke 6:43–44. Here the conclusion of M. S. Enslin appears valid that though "this word now stands in the mouth of John the Baptist, it is highly probable . . . that it, like all of John's reported messages, is in essence a word of Jesus, subsequently transferred to that one's "Christianized" forerunner" (*The Prophet from Nazareth,* p. 107).

18. Possibly a Semitic idiom, this oft-repeated summons has an apocalyptic ring to it. If not actually the words of Jesus, the cry expresses the urgency with which He saw His mission (Matt. 11:15, 13:9, 13:43; Mark 4:9, 4:23; Luke 8:8, 14:35).

19. J. B. Phillips, *When God Was Man* (New York: Abingdon Press, 1958), pp. 10–11.

8 The Rising Wind

"For I tell you, unless your righteousness exceeds that of the scribes and Pharisees, you will never enter the kingdom of heaven."

—Matt. 5:20

And as he sat at table in the house, many tax collectors and sinners came and sat down with Jesus and his disciples.

And when the Pharisees saw this, they said to his disciples, "Why does your teacher eat with tax collectors and sinners?"

But when he heard it, he said, "Those who are well have no need of a physician, but those who are sick. Go and learn what this means, 'I desire mercy, and not sacrifice.' For I came not to call the righteous, but sinners."

—Matt. 9:10–13

The portrayal of Jesus in the Gospels is that of a fiercely independent personality. At the close of the Sermon on the Mount, Matthew states that the crowds were amazed because Jesus taught "as one who had authority, and not as their scribes" (7:28–29), a reaction that John compresses into a report by Temple police, "No man ever spoke like this man" (7:46).

Where did the power of Jesus come from, the freedom and spiritual energy so animating His teachings as to leave His listeners speechless? Mark records that immediately following the baptism of Jesus, the Spirit of God "drove" Him into the wilderness where He was "tempted by Satan" (1:12). That lesser aims and conflicting desires returned to tempt Jesus is hinted but (Mark 3:31; 8:32–33; 14:36), but each time he emerges from the testing on a higher plane of emotional stability and response. Sprung from the common people by prophetic fervor, He feels led by God to assume a momentous task, and thus answerable only to the Spirit. "The wind blows where it wills, and you hear the sound of it, but you do not know whence it comes or whither it goes: so it is with everyone born of the Spirit." [1]

The truth originates with the evangelist John rather than with Jesus, but this in no way undermines the fact that the Spirit of God moves unrestrained and often in unexpected ways. It does so in Jesus. Like a child's Fourth of July sparkler, He burns with a white-hot intensity of concentrated drive and conviction. Fragments of His teaching blaze with this intensity, as do also His debates with adversaries. The approach of Jesus to His task is that of an individual working against time. He must prepare men quickly for the age soon to dawn. His people must repent and begin to live with confident trust in God, an attitude of faith impossible so long as it is hampered by a reliance upon ritual. Faith is not a ritual to be analyzed, but a relationship to be enjoyed. Love is an invincible force.

Sifting through the Law and the Prophets, therefore, Jesus lifts from the altar of past inspiration the fire rather than the ashes. The result is a Torah simplified but in many ways more strict. The essentials laid bare are such as everyday folk can understand. Let love for God be spontaneous. Let service be cheerful and willing. Let forgiveness be unlimited. Let hatred be outlawed save toward evil. Let justice and mercy be practiced even before Temple sacrifice. Cut off the dishonest hand, gouge out the lustful eye rather than be denied entrance to the Kingdom. Repent! Believe! Rejoice! Watch! Pray! Bear good fruit! In such a vein does Jesus speak out of Himself what He feels sown by the Spirit within.

The spiritual independence of Jesus reveals itself as we contrast Him with members of existing groups. One group was the Sadducees, but, while agreeing with them that the traditions of the Pharisees were not equal in authority with the Mosaic Law, Jesus differed sharply from the Sadducees in outlook and motive. They rejected the Pharisaic claim out of jealousy; Jesus rejected it for moral and religious reasons. They were reactionary, He prophetic.

Unlike the Essenes, with whom the Dead Sea Scrolls are associated, Jesus was no monastic. It has been suggested He was. He reverenced the Torah; He went apart to pray in deserted places; He disapproved of Temple abuses. And yet Jesus does not fit the mold of the Jewish monks who despaired of human society as too evil to redeem and Temple worship as too corrupt to uphold. Religion to Jesus was a dynamic force operating fully while people labored in their daily vocation. The ideals of faith and righteousness were obtainable through participation in society rather than by escape from it. And so, unlike the Essenes, Jesus did not encourage His followers to sever relations with humanity.

With the scribes and Pharisees, of course, Jesus shared most in common. He is said to have lauded the affirmation of a scribe who grasped the essential content of the Law (Mark 12:34). In company with the Pharisees, Jesus believed in the resurrection of the dead and the reality of a future life. He championed righteousness, which was their passion and goal. A number of their ethical principles dot His teachings. And yet Jesus does not entirely fit this system of thought and practice either. In the eyes of pedantic scribes and Pharisees, He showed an upsetting originality. Jesus was too unpredictable for scholars to relax with, too lenient toward the *'am ha-arez*, too sociable toward "sinners."

From this we might assume that Jesus mirrored at all points the mind and mood of the *'am ha-arez*. By His lowly origin and prophetic inclination, He was one of them. In Him shone traits typical of the better northern provincial: a "hardheaded realism, broadmindedness, the common touch, a certain rather prickly defiance when dealing with scornfully superior Judaeans." [2] To Hillel, the celebrated rabbi, all *'am ha-arez* were ungodly,[3] but not to Jesus. His own religion was fundamentally that of the best of them, in whom a love of God compensated for a lack of systematic theology, and faith for meticulous study of the Law.

Still, while compassionate, Jesus was not blind to the spiritual faults of His brethren. They were not always right or God-fearing. Upon those evil among them, as well as those good, God caused the sun to rise, the rain to fall. Often conservative for the sake of conservatism, they acted more out of custom than conviction. Jesus, on the other hand, appears to have acted from religious motives. Those *'am ha-arez* wishing to avoid Temple taxes found little encouragement in His censure of Pharisees who tithed, for it was not the payment of tithes that Jesus criticized but Pharisaic neglect of moral duties—"justice and mercy and faith" (Matt. 23:23). In reported disputes over eating grain or healing on the Sabbath, the concern of Jesus is again moral rather than ritualistic (Mark 2:23–27; 3:1–5). Hence the deduction is probably correct that, though sympathetic toward His countrymen, Jesus did not belong to a Galilean or agrarian party as such.[4]

Inhabitants of Galilee included Zealots also, those red-blooded Jewish resistance fighters whose courage often as not led to a Roman cross. Was Jesus a Zealot? Or a "fellow traveler"? Or, while in agreement with various Zealot aims, did Jesus once more strike out upon an independent course?

Only in the last quarter-century has the way been open for investigation of Jesus' relationship to the Jewish underground. Such an investigation had long been unpursued because Christians on both sides of the Atlantic abhorred any inference that Jesus was subversive. This reaction was to be expected. Prior to 1940, guerrillas in Latin America, Asia, and Africa had consistently appeared as anything but patriotic in western eyes by their efforts to topple colonial establishments. During the Second World War, however, this western view shifted. S. G. F.

Brandon asserts that "the admiration and encouragement given to 'resistance groups' in various Nazi-occupied lands . . . stirred a new and sympathetic interest in the Zealots" which "is beginning to show itself in New Testament study." [5] Let us look, then, at what has been and still is a murky subject for examination.

The origin of Zealotism would seem to lie in the raids led by a Galilean "bandit" named Hezekiah. At this time—about 47–46 B.C.—Herod (later called "the Great") was governor of Galilee. Since he at all costs had to retain Roman favor through preserving peace in his area, Herod knew that Hezekiah must go. Chasing the rebels back into their caves, he ordered them smoked out and their leader executed. Guerrilla depredations throughout Galilee, however, did not end there; as it turned out, Hezekiah was but the first of a dynastic succession of rebel leaders. It was one of Hezekiah's sons—Judas of Gamala—who led the Sepphoris uprising; and Menahem, the son of Judas, in A.D. 66 launched the revolt that left Jerusalem demolished. Significantly, when Roman troops broke into the last Zealot fortress at Masada seven years later, they found virtually no one left alive to kill or enslave: the Zealot commander, Eleazar—another descendent of Judas—had persuaded 960 men, women, and children to choose suicide rather than surrender. The Zealot history consequently extends across 125 years of bloody strife, the mid-third of which is the lifespan of Jesus.

This fatal procession of events gives the impression that Zealots were either foolhardy or insane. It must be remembered, though, that in first-century Judaism, religion and politics were inseparable. The soil given as the Promised Land remained sacred despite the tread of heathen feet. The Jews continued to regard themselves as the Chosen People. Holy destiny dictated that Israel be restored as a theocracy under Yahweh, as "a light to the nations" [that is, Gentiles] that His salvation might reach to the ends of the earth (Isa. 49:6). If the great day tarried, Jewish unfaithfulness was responsible. Let the land, therefore, be purged. Let the Torah be taught with zeal. Let passion for righteousness burn bright in every heart and home. Let there be "no king but Yahweh!" Then, and only then, would Yahweh send help, and the hated Romans and their hirelings be driven out.

Zealot aims were thus those of the Pharisees in regard to personal righteousness and a theocratic Israel. Only on strategy did Pharisee and Zealot differ, the Zealot taking the road of sword, ambush, terrorism, and assassination, while the Pharisee foreswore armed resistance and resorted to prayer, fasting, exhortation, and purification. In the words of S. G. F. Brandon, the Zealots

> uncompromisingly sought to maintain Israel's absolute conformity to the Torah and its complete loyalty to Yahweh as its sovereign lord. To secure these ideals, they were prepared to resort to violent action against both the Romans, who occupied their land, and those of their countrymen whose acceptance of Roman rule was particularly notable. . . .[6]

> But it was not in their own strength that the Zealots trusted; their trust lay in the God who had miraculously delivered their ancestors from slavery in Egypt. The history of their people, recorded in a holy scripture, was a veritable *Heilsgeschichte,* abounding with thrilling accounts of how Yahweh had saved those who faithfully and courageously had withstood the impious heathen—from Joshua to Judas Maccabaeus, long and inspiring was the roll of Israel's heroes, whose faith and daring had been so signally rewarded by their God. It is, therefore, a necessary inference that Judas and Saddok, when they called upon their people to withstand the Roman demand, also believed that the kingdom of God was at hand. Even Josephus admits that they expected God's succour, and it is likely that, no less vividly than Jesus, they might have envisaged the intervention of twelve legions of angels.[7]

These revolutionaries were part of the Galilean scene in which Jesus grew up. Most likely He knew townsmen in Nazareth who, if not Zealots, were related to Zealots. Survivors of the Sepphoris defeat may have stayed on in the town after taking refuge there. Underground couriers might easily have stopped overnight for food and rest.

Later, as Jesus moved about the lake country, His exposure to Zealot activity would have· increased. The Roman army camps on the coast were more distant now, the Zealot staging areas across the Jordan nearer. News of Roman punitive actions reached Him. One of these Luke mentions: "There were some present at that very time who told him of the Galileans whose blood Pilate had mingled with their Temple sacrifices" (13:1). The reference assumes added import when it is realized how often the names "Galilean" and "Zealot" were used interchangeably.

The fact that one, if not several, of Jesus' disciples were Zealots or former Zealots appears indisputable. Matthew follows Mark in concealing this connection by referring to a certain Simon as "the Cananaean," but Luke identifies the same Simon as he "who was called the Zealot." (Matt. 10:4; Mark 3:18; Luke 6:15). Unless short swords can be proven normal pilgrim accessories (Luke 22:38), the disciples' carrying of them looks suspicious. So also does the involvement of Barabbas in the Passion story (Matt. 27:16; Mark 15:7; Luke 23:18–19), the charge of sedition ("forbidding us to give tribute to Caesar," (Luke 23:2), and the crucifixion of Jesus between two "robbers" (Matt. 27:38; Mark 15:27; Luke 23:33).[8]

But was Jesus actually a Zealot? That He was politically sensitive seems clear. That He met and associated with known revolutionaries is likely. That Zealots were active in Jerusalem when He arrived and that these firebrands would exploit to their advantage the popularity of Jesus (and any demonstration His presence might excite) is plausible. Modern history illustrates this tactic. Recalling the sanitation workers' march through Memphis in 1968, Coretta Scott King tells how her husband "had gone no more than a few blocks when he heard crashing glass and the sounds of rocks and bottles being thrown from the back of the line. It has generally been agreed that the trouble had not been started by the marchers but by gangs of young men who, using the parade as a cover, hurled rocks through windows and dodged in and out of the ranks." [9]

To conclude from such evidence, however, that Jesus was a Zealot cannot, to my mind, be supported. Even S. G. F. Brandon does not go that far.[10] Instead, Jesus appears as independent of the Zealots as of any of the other groups mentioned, and in substantiation of this view at least three lines of reasoning may be posed.

First, the nonviolent teachings of Jesus are to be considered, teachings now so familiar as to require only phrases to recall them to mind: "Blessed are the peacemakers . . . do not resist one who is evil . . . strikes you on the right cheek . . . go with him two miles . . . love your enemies." (Sermon on the Mount: Matt. 5:9, 39, 41, 44). These teachings, Dr. Brandon contends, are an outgrowth of the Church's need to picture Jesus as in no way a political menace to Rome, but "the innocent victim of the malice of the Jewish leaders." [11] Mark starts the Gospels down this road when he depicts Jesus as so transcendental in nature and message as to be unconcerned about the Jewish political crisis. Since the Jewish revolt of A.D. 66 occurred only shortly before Mark wrote, it would have been extremely dangerous to have presented Jesus as any other sort of savior to a Gentile audience.

What Dr. Brandon states may very well be true. In the past, the glib acceptance of the Sermon on the Mount, without thought to the circumstances under which that collection of sayings moved from word of mouth to inscribed papyrus, has reduced greatly the historical value of many published "Lives." In and of themselves, therefore, the pacifist sayings attributed to Jesus are not conclusive proof of His freedom from revolutionary excesses. And yet is the historicity of these teachings to be devalued solely because Christians needed to project a nonmilitant image when the Gospels of Matthew and Luke were assembled? To argue that such teachings were fabricated or doctored to meet a later emergency is to insult logic as much as Christian sensibilities. May it not be argued just as convincingly that teaching fragments existed which strengthened the view that Jesus was unjustly condemned, and which the Evangelists seized upon to control the angry frustration of persecuted Christians at a later date?

Another argument in support of Jesus' noninvolvement in Zealot fanaticism is the apparent nature of the Jerusalem Church. This congregation warrants scrutiny because at the start it counted eleven of the original Twelve among its members and therefore may be thought expressive of its crucified leader's mood. If highly Zealot in attitude and program, this church would indicate that Jesus was as well. And this is the tack which Dr. Brandon takes.

> Seeing, then, that there is no reason why the Jewish Christians should have differed in their attitude to the Roman rule from that taken by the Zealots, we should expect that a certain sympathy would have existed between them. . . . The fact . . . that Jesus included a Zealot among his twelve disciples, and the fact that he is never recorded to have condemned the Zealots or their principles, constitute evidence of the greatest importance. . . . Such inferences, which are not only legitimate but compelling, authorise our regarding the Jewish Christians as a party closely allied by sympathy and outlook with the Zealots. Their chief difference was that they believed that the restoration of the kingdom to Israel would be affected by the return of Jesus as the Messiah. They would thus have constituted a kind of para-Zealot movement: possibly many of their adherents such as Simon the Zealot . . . were also members of the Zealot party or moved freely in both groups.[12]

This scholar then asks "whether the Jewish Christians also shared the Zealot belief in active resistance," and concludes that "surviving tradition gives no clear indication in either direction." [13] The most his investigation will permit is the conjecture that Zealotism had its strongholds at first in rural areas beyond Jerusalem, and only about A.D. 63 began to operate in the city; that, besides dedicated members living a nomadic existence, many Zealot sympathizers lived normal lives in towns and villages, operating clandestinely as opportunity arose; that Jesus and His disciples lived a nomadic existence so that only after the Resurrection experiences was the headquarters of the movement established in Jerusalem where it remained until the catastrophe of A.D. 70.

If true, where does this leave us? In Brandon's words, we are left to conclude that "the Christian community in the city could scarcely have engaged, if it had been so disposed, in active opposition to the Romans or their Jewish cooperators." [14] Why? The reasons are self-evident: because conditions in Judea at the time of the Crucifixion had not yet reached that state which three decades later touched off a paroxysm of Zealot fury; and because the disciples after the death of Jesus were in no position to engage in armed resistance.

Completely unstrung, the disciples raced homeward to the relative safety of Galilee. There, after several days of numbing grief, first Peter and then the others "saw the Lord." [15] The ensuing experience of glad recognition did not come, however, without the disciples' first bleeding heavy drops of doubt and remorse. Justin Martyr recounts[16] less than a century later how the disciples, after Jesus rose from the dead, repented of their flight when He was crucified. The Gospels, though, in their eagerness to show the disciples transformed and fearless, return them to Jerusalem unrealistically soon and in order to accomplish this have to play down their emotional trauma. Matthew nevertheless states that while some were led by the reappearances of Jesus to worship Him, "some doubted" (28:17). Most revealing, though, is the dejected reply of the disciples on the Emmaus Road. Through them, in this beautiful story Luke allows the full disillusionment of a broken dream to appear, the early Church speaking through Cleopas and his companion as it struggles to fathom a nightmare.

> Then one of them, named Cleopas, answered him, "Are you the only visitor to Jerusalem who does not know the things that have happened there in these days?" And he said to them, "What things?" And they said to him, "Concerning Jesus of Nazareth, who was a prophet mighty in deed and word before God and all the people, and how our chief priests and rulers delivered him up to be condemned to death, and crucified him. But we had hoped that he was the one to redeem Israel (Luke 24:18–21).

The return of the disciples to Jerusalem thus came about only after a natural interlude of sorrow and adjustment. Did they then link up with the Jewish underground? Not likely. Emotionally and spiritually they had their hands full assimilating the experience they had been through and convincing others of its validity. In their fellowship and work they went unmolested by the authorities, because Judaism was a ceremonial religion and as long as a Jew conformed to the Law he could teach openly in the Temple with considerable freedom.

The fellowship of the disciples with each other and their risen Lord was warm and intimate. In the breaking of the common loaf, He was revealed. In opening the Scriptures, their hearts burned with rewarded expectation. They were a band of hope, confident that the future would vindicate their belief in Jesus as the Messiah, risen and glorified. Study of their message summarized in Acts (2:14–36 and 3:12–26) shows it to be futuristic—near future, to be sure, but futuristic all the same. The preaching of the Apostle Peter is an eschatological proclamation rather than a call to arms: "Repent, therefore, and turn again, that your sins may be blotted out, that times of refreshing may come from the presence of the Lord, and that he may send the Christ appointed for you, Jesus, whom heaven must receive until the time for establishing all that God spoke by the mouth of his holy prophets from of old" (Acts 3:19–21).[17]

To believe, therefore, that the Jerusalem Church actively joined the Zealots in revolutionary plotting appears unjustifiable. Before long, James (Jacob)—the brother of Jesus— emerged as the leader of the Jerusalem Church, a significant development, as it turned out, because that church soon became quietistic and nonviolent rather than vengeful and frenzied.[18] During the mid-sixties, this situation may well have altered. As Dr. Brandon suggests,[19] some Jerusalem Christians probably joined in the Zealots' final rush to arms. The Church there then perished in the flaming city. This may be—but that was three decades after the period which concerns us.

The third and final argument in support of a nonviolent, non-Zealot Jesus originates with Shirley Jackson Case. The passing of forty years since the publication of his article "Jesus and Sepphoris" has lessened none of its persuasiveness.

> Perhaps the influence of Sepphoris is to be seen in an even more pronounced degree in shaping Jesus' attitude toward the Roman government. The people of Sepphoris and its vicinity were three-quarters of a century earlier than the people of Jerusalem in learning by sad experience the utter futility of a revolution against Rome. When at the time of his first insurrection Judas had taken possession of the royal treasures and arms at Sepphoris, evidently the citizens were not unsympathetic with his action, for when the Romans suppressed the revolution they burned the city and enslaved the inhabitants. But the residents of the new city were distinctly opposed to all revolutionary movements. Not even its Jewish population could be persuaded to take up arms against Rome. When at the time of the census Judas instigated a fresh revolt he had to find a new center for his operations. Again, during the early stages of the uprising of 66 A.D., when Josephus was busy fortifying Galilee to resist the Roman armies, he found the citizens of Sepphoris entirely out of sympathy with his enterprise, although the city was recognized by all concerned as quite properly a part of the Jewish domains. Notwithstanding the fact that it

was strategically situated and could have offered formidable resistance, when the Romans appeared upon the scene, Sepphoris, with its surrounding villages, immediately declared itself opposed to the policy of revolution. The citizens pledged fidelity to the Romans and were given a Roman garrison for their protection.

That shortly before the year 30 A.D. a carpenter from the neighboring village of Nazareth should have had his own attitude toward the Roman government influenced by this characteristic psychology of the people of Sepphoris is, of course, only a conjecture. But the attitude which this city and its outlying villages took in the year 66 A.D. had been in force for three quarters of a century. After the restoration by Antipas the inhabitants realized how futile had been the attempt of their predecessors to wrest independence from the Romans by force of arms. Those persons who participated in the work of restoration, whether laborers, merchants or residents in general, had no desire that history should repeat itself. It required no very extraordinary powers of foresight on their part to perceive that further revolution would issue only in a new disaster to life and property. But in holding to this attitude, they were entirely out of harmony with other sections of Galilee, where Judas and his kinsmen continued the agitation that issued in the uprising of 66 A.D.[20]

This would indicate that while Jews in the Nazareth area lived with hope of divine deliverance, they differed with their Jewish countrymen elsewhere as how best to realize that hope. If this is so, then an attitude of nonresistance on the part of Jesus would be natural. Such an ethic would epitomize the only sane course to take in a country burdened by a ruthless army of occupation, inescapable taxes, and corrupt princes and priests. This position, though, exacted its price. The enemies of Jesus adroitly used it against Him by publicly raising the issue of Roman taxation. His response, "Render to Caesar the things that are Caesar's," was not satisfactory to many who otherwise might have rallied to His standard. Yet Jesus persevered in His belief that armed revolt was self-defeating. The lesson of Sepphoris was not lost on Him, His childhood memory of smoke and crosses a perpetual reminder that they who take the sword will perish by the sword. The Kingdom of God must come another way.

Zealots, Essenes, Sadducees, *'am ha-arez,* scribes, and Pharisees: all are part of the Gospel drama, although some are left standing upstage in the shadows as if they played no role, even indirectly, in the life of Jesus. Herodians and Gentiles are part of the cast. They, no less than others, were on the scene when Jesus called for repentance. Before His meteoric career burned itself out in the abrasive, unreceptive atmosphere of Jerusalem, members of each class and group came to know Jesus and He them, however fleeting their contact.

And yet, as we have emphasized over and over again, Jesus was distinctively Himself and made His own way. Without fear of contamination, He mixed freely with publicans and "sinners," the sick and outcast. As a Galilean He conversed with foreigners. Not every heathen gave himself to prurient living, a fact the Apostle Paul was to acknowledge (Rom. 2:12–16). On the other hand, while some Gentiles showed a commendable sense of morality and faith, many did not, and, if Matthew is correct, Jesus used them as object lessons in reverse. He spurned inflated prayer—"In praying do not heap up empty phrases as the Gentiles do" (Matt. 6:7); He rejected materialistic fears— "Do not be anxious, saying, 'What shall we eat?' or 'What shall we drink?' or 'What shall we wear?' For the Gentiles seek all these things" (Matt. 6:32); and He renounced the overbearing spirit— "The rulers of the Gentiles lord it over them, and their great men exercise authority over them. It shall not be so among you" (Matt. 20:25). If not the very words of Jesus, the viewpoint expressed is that which might be anticipated in one of lowly birth who deeply and overwhelmingly felt the presence of God.

Such bold independence soon builds its opposition. The followers of Herod Antipas began casting wary eyes at the crowds attracted by the young Galilian. The Herodian police in Capernaum no doubt reported His preaching to their superiors in Tiberias and awaited instructions.

The Pharisees grew alarmed. At first the enthusiasm with which this Galilean called for repentance and righteousness had delighted them. They had been as much surprised by Him as others were. Despite their usual reserve, the Pharisees found that something in His delivery gripped them; it was not the message which made the man so much as the man the message. His conviction was overpowering. Only later, after reflecting among themselves apart from the sway of His personality, did the Pharisees realize how irreducibly opposed their approach to religion was to His. If He had His way, Jesus would lead them where they dare not follow. Besides, His blunt replies were humiliating, He who had never studied under the rabbis. But what could one expect of a Galilean *'am ha-arez* who was convinced that His inspiration was equal to that of the Torah!

Meanwhile Jesus Himself was changing. The Gospels offer scant indication of this, but if we are to accept Jesus as truly human, then we must accept as well the fact that the dynamics which operate in any human being operated in Him. One reason why the humanity of Jesus fails to impress modern readers of the Gospels more is because the adoration of the Church would not permit character development in Him beyond His wilderness temptation (unless the Gethsemane scene is to be so considered).[21] We may be sure, however, that character growth did take place, that Jesus changed His mind and recast His convictions. Despite tradition's attempt to freeze the personality and character of Jesus at an early point in His mission, the impression comes that His attitude toward Mosaic Law grew ever more flexible.

But, it may be objected, what are we then to make of the statement, "Think not that I have come to abolish the law and the prophets; I have come not to abolish them but to fulfill them" (Matt. 5:17)? That is decidedly not a flexible statement.

Nor are those statements which follow: "For truly, I say to you, till heaven and earth pass away, not an iota, not a dot, will pass from the law until all is accomplished. Whoever then relaxes one of the least of these commandments and teaches men so, shall be called least in the kingdom of heaven; but he who does them and teaches them shall be called great." Some scholars question the authenticity of this material. They are convinced it represents the desire of the early Church either to tone down the radical teachings that immediately follow, or to ward off later attacks of Pharisees upon the Church. Another view, however, is possible; the conservative statement may be genuine. If so, it belongs to the opening phase of Jesus' ministry. The positions of Jesus regarding murder and adultery may be reconciled with His "Come not to abolish" statement, but not the positions He takes on divorce, oaths, retaliation, and loving one's enemies (to say nothing of ceremonial cleanliness and Sabbath observance!).[22]

Thus the suspicion takes root that the attitude of Jesus toward the Law and Pharisees changed with time and controversy. Whereas He once felt the Law expressive of God's unchanging will and the error of the Pharisees only that of observing it too externally, Jesus became more critical. Gradually He came to believe that a number of Mosaic teachings actually obstructed the leading of the Spirit to which he was committed. Fitting well with this conclusion is the portrayal of Jesus as a man of prayer, for no doubt He underwent more than one Gethsemane spiritually before that which He knew outside Jerusalem.

Seen from this perspective, the controversy between Jesus and the Pharisees was inevitable. Those scribes of the Pharisees who followed Him at the start soon fell away when He commenced eating with tax collectors and "sinners."[23] After this breach, the polarization grew steadily. The Pharisees "watched him" to see if He would heal a withered hand on the Sabbath, and He "looked around at them with anger" (Mark 3:1-5). They heard Jesus forgive sins, and objected, "It is blasphemy!

Who can forgive sins but God alone?" (Mark 1:1–12). As months of skirmishing passed, His criticism in turn sharpened:

> You Pharisees cleanse the outside of the cup and of the dish, but inside you are full of extortion and wickedness. You fools! Did not he who made the outside make the inside also? (Luke 11:39–40)

Finally came the accusation which caused Jesus to counter-attack: the Pharisees called Him a partner of Beelzebul, prince of demons.

> Every kingdom divided against itself is laid waste, and house falls upon house. And if Satan also is divided against himself, how will his kingdom stand? For you say that I cast out demons by Beelzebul. And if I cast out demons by Beelzebul, by whom do your sons cast them out? Therefore they shall be your judges. But if it is by the finger of God that I cast out demons, then the kingdom of God has come upon you. (Luke 11:17–20)

Such clashes as recorded in the Gospels unquestionably reflect the post-Resurrection experience of Christians and their persecution by Pharisees, but there is equally little question that in these bitter exchanges were the wood and nails of which a cross was made. The curiosity of the Pharisees turned first to caution, then to fear, and at last to hate. Withdrawing from Jesus, they approached Herodians whom they found also angry, but for political reasons. By themselves the Pharisees could do little in Galilee against the troublesome Nazarene. Allied with the aristocratic followers of Antipas, they became dangerous.

For His part, Jesus turned southward. Already He may have sensed that the crowds surging about Him would not be enough. To go to Jerusalem could mean His death, but go He must. The Temple awaited cleansing, and its priestly elite, judgment. Long before in the nation's history, Nathan the prophet had denounced the sins of his king, saying, "You are the man. Why have you despised the word of the Lord and done evil in his sight?" Now He—Jesus of Nazareth—would denounce the sins of these present rulers and awaken in them a saving shame. Let them heed His call to repentance, confess with David, "I have sinned against the Lord," and this crooked generation might still right itself morally in time to meet the Day of the Lord with head erect. The wind of the Spirit was rising. If only those in Jerusalem could be made to feel it, and respond! And so, determined to follow the Spirit where it led, Jesus set His face to go to Jerusalem. (Luke 9:51).

NOTES

1. This quotation from the Fourth Gospel (3:8) includes an interesting play upon words, the Greek noun used for "wind" and "spirit" being the same.

2. Jean Steinmann, *The Life of Jesus* (Boston: Little, Brown and Co., 1963), pp. 20–21.

3. Pirke Aboth 2, 6 (Mishnah).

4. Sherman E. Johnson, "Jesus and First-Century Galilee," in Schmauch, *Memoriam Ernst Lohmeyer*, p. 77.

5. S. G. F. Brandon, *Jesus and the Zealots: A Study of the Political Factor in Primitive Christianity* (New York: Chas. Scribner's and Sons, 1968), p. 24.

6. Brandon, *Jesus and the Zealots,* pp. 46–47.

7. Ibid. p. 51.

8. Roman readers, for obvious reasons, considered Zealots to be cutthroats and thieves rather than patriots. Josephus thus refers to the rebels as "bandits" in his *War of the Jews* in the same manner in which two U. S. Marines did concerning the Viet Cong in a 1968 conversation with me.

9. C. S. King, *My Life with Martin Luther King, Jr.* (New York: Holt, Rinehart and Winston, Inc., 1969), pp. 309–10.

10. Samuel Sandmel is mistaken in his assessment of *Jesus and the Zealots* when he states that Dr. Brandon asserts "in the plainest terms that Jesus was a Zealot, a member of the activist group that spurred the succession of rebellions against Rome which culminated in the destruction of the Temple" (see "Pacifist or Zealot?" *Saturday Review*, Jan.

4, 1969, pp. 87–89). Accurately *Time* (Jan. 3, 1969, pp. 54–55) observes that "Brandon carefully avoids saying that Jesus was a Zealot himself, but cites evidence suggesting that he was sympathetic to their cause."

11. Brandon, *Jesus and the Zealots*, p. 323.

12. Ibid., pp. 200–201.

13. Ibid., pp. 201–202.

14. Ibid., p. 202.

15. The fact that the Resurrection appearances first occurred in Galilee rather than Jerusalem quickly became so firmly and widely accepted among Christians that Mark could not displace it with the more popular story of the empty Jerusalem tomb. Hence the women at the tomb are given a heaven-sent message to reconcile the discrepancy and preserve both the Galilean and Jerusalem versions: "But go, tell his disciples and Peter that he is going before you to Galilee; there you will see him, as he told you" (16:7). See also Mark 14:28.

16. Justin Martyr, *Dialogue*, 106.

17. Frederick C. Grant, *The Earliest Gospel* (Nashville: Abingdon Press, 1943), pp. 15–17.

18. In Acts (1:14; 2:42–47), Luke undoubtedly offers an overly harmonious picture of the early Jerusalem Church, but there is no reason to challenge the characterization of a pietistic, orthodox pattern of life within it.

19. Brandon, *Jesus and the Zealots*, pp. 216–20.

20. S. J. Case, "Jesus and Sepphoris," *Journal of Biblical Literature* 45 (1926), pp. 20–21.

21. *Temptation:* Matt. 4:1–11; Luke 4:1–13. *Gethsemane:* Matt. 26:36–42; Mark 14:32–39; Luke 22:41–44.

22. *Murder:* Matt. 5:21–26. *Adultery:* Matt. 5:27–30. *Divorce:* Matt. 5:31–32; Mark 10:11–12; Luke 16:18; Matt. 19:3–9; Mark 10:2–12. *Oaths:* Matt. 5:33–37; 23:16–22. *Retaliation:* Matt. 5:38–42; Luke 6:29–31. *Love enemies:* Matt. 5:43–47; Luke 6:27–28, 32–36. *Ceremonial cleanliness:* Matt. 15:1–12; Mark 7:1–8. *Sabbath observance:* Matt. 12:1–8; Mark 2:23–28; Luke 6:1–5.

23. Maurice Goguel cites, "Many of the people followed him, even some of the scribes of the Pharisees" as a preferable rendering of Mark 2:15–16 (*Jesus and the Origins of Christianity*, vol. 2, p. 345, footnote 1).

9 The Storm Breaks

And they were on the road, going up to Jerusalem, and Jesus was walking ahead of them; . . . and those who followed were afraid.
—Mark 10:32

And many spread their garments on the road, and others spread leafy branches which they had cut from the fields. And those who went before and those who followed cried out, "Hosanna! Blessed be he who comes in the name of the Lord! Blessed be the kingdom of our father David that is coming!"
—Mark 11:8–10

And he entered the temple and began to drive out those who sold and those who bought in the temple, and he overturned the tables of the money changers and the seats of those who sold pigeons; and he would not allow any one to carry anything through the temple.
—Mark 11:15–16

The glimpse Mark offers of Jesus on His way to Jerusalem has generally been accepted. Having prophesied His death there, Jesus advances toward certain disaster. He is a lonely figure of a man, withdrawn and uncommunicative. Behind Him come His disciples who, despite their continued loyalty, are fearful as to what the future may hold. The solidarity they have known is broken now by jealous arguments.

This impression Mark gives of the final journey is deliberate. Immediately after the confession of Peter at Caesarea Philippi, Mark has Jesus begin to teach His disciples "that the Son of man must suffer many things, and be rejected by the elders and the chief priests and the scribes, and be killed, and after three days rise again" (Mark 8:30), a prediction that, though twice repeated, still leaves the disciples puzzled.

I say that Mark *has* Jesus so prophesy and His disciples so react, because from a historical viewpoint the prophecies give every appearance of being artificially imposed. Mark uses them to bring his account of the final days into agreement with theological beliefs already upheld in the Church. Thus it was necessary that the disciples appear uncomprehending; otherwise they—who except for Judas had become revered Apostles by the time Mark wrote—would have been placed in an embarrassing light: Why, if they knew what was coming, did they nothing to avoid it?

At the same time, Mark wishes to prepare his readers for the Passion story. He therefore has Jesus predict his suffering and death no less than three times,[1] all this in agreement with the early Christian conviction that Jesus as the Son of God knew in advance what was in store for Him at Jerusalem and that He was "delivered up according to the definite plan and fore-knowledge of God" (Acts 2:23). What could be more inconceivable than that Jesus the Christ should have died without an inkling of the glorious triumph awaiting Him beyond the Cross? The thought—too horrible for Christian contemplation—was rejected.

This leads us to suspect that Mark has made his portrayal of Jesus at this point in His life excessively gloomy. If Jesus had misgivings as to how long He would survive in Jerusalem, those misgivings are too masked now by theological assumptions to be distinguishable. We can only guess at His state of mind. He was undoubtedly aware of growing danger; danger had been His traveling companion for months. The spies of Herod Antipas had been so active and the threat of assassination or capture so acute that from time to time Jesus was forced into seclusion outside Galilee until Herodian searches were called off. Meanwhile John the Baptist had been swept up by the Herodian police on the Jordan. How much greater, therefore, were the chances that Jesus would soon be disposed of in Jerusalem.

To say that Jesus recognized the dangers, however, is a far cry from saying He had a martyr complex. He went to Jerusalem to *act,* not to die. Life rather than martyrdom obsessed Him—the life of His people who must repent quickly in order to complete their divine mission. Hope thus burned bright in Jesus. Many continued to welcome His message; the crowds had not soured and drifted away.[2] Having brought Him this far, God would surely continue to inspire and guide him.

> The Spirit of the Lord God is upon me,
>   because the Lord has anointed me
> to bring good tidings to the afflicted;
>   he has sent me to bind up the brokenhearted,
> to proclaim liberty to the captives,
>   and the opening of the prison to those who
>   are bound;
> to proclaim the year of the Lord's favor,
>   and the day of vengeance of our God;
>   to comfort all who mourn;
> to grant to those who mourn in Zion—
>   to give them a garland instead of ashes,
> the oil of gladness instead of mourning,
>   the mantle of praise instead of a faint
>   spirit;
> that they may be called oaks of righteousness,
>   the planting of the Lord, that he may be
>   glorified.
> (Isa. 61:1–3)

Flaming, confident hope turned Jesus southward. What place had morbid despair in Him? His trust lay in God, God who had caused Isaiah to see what others missed, to grasp as truth what others ignored.

> I will greatly rejoice in the Lord,
>   my soul shall exalt in my God. . . .
> For as the earth brings forth its shoots,
>   and as a garden causes what is sown in it
>   to spring up,
> so the Lord God will cause righteousness and
>   praise to spring forth before all the
>   nations.
> For Zion's sake I will not keep silent,
>   and for Jerusalem's sake I will not rest,
> until her vindication goes forth as brightness,
>   and her salvation as a burning torch.
> (Isa. 61:10, 11; 62:1)

Empowered by the Spirit, Jesus came to Jerusalem, but He came not to "Ride on, ride on in majesty! In lowly pomp ride on to die." He came to preach and heal and do whatever else promised to bring His countrymen to spiritual readiness, to repentance, to a resumption of their unique mission among the nations.

His task was Herculean. He could not have pitted His courage and ability against greater odds. The Herodian aristocracy was adamant in its opposition to any messianic personality who with his preachments might upset the established order. Emperor Tiberius had replaced Archelaus with a Roman governor, but the one-time supporters of Archelaus still resided in their villas outside Jerusalem hoping for a change.

During the reign of Herod the Great, there had at least been a semblance of home rule. Taxes then had passed through Herodian hands, and construction contracts were profitable for those who won and kept Herod's favor. Now all this was past. With the death of Herod the Great and the ouster of his son, Judean taxes flowed directly to the imperial coffers, and—except at the Temple—building slowed to a crawl. The rise of any prophet would only serve to tighten Roman control and delay the time when, if things quieted down, Tiberius might be induced to return a Herod to power in Judea.

The Sadducees no less resisted change. Backed by wealthy families, they stepped into the vacuum left by the fall of Archelaus. Through arrangements with Rome, the Sadducean party retained control of the Temple and, by means of it, the power structure of Jerusalem. Both local and Temple police were at the Sadducees' command. The party held a majority of seats in the Sanhedrin, the supreme court of Judaism. Nearly all the priests administering Temple rites were party members.

The dominance of the Sadducees went further: substantial monetary resources were at their disposal. The Temple, like a brilliant iceberg, could be seen a long distance. And, like an iceberg, the Temple concealed beneath its surface more than appeared above. Behind its marble exterior and year-round activity lay great commercial interests. This was not unusual. In the ancient world, banking sprang up wherever states began minting coins. Out of the confusion of uncoordinated local coinage came the first bankers who, seated at their small tables, exchanged one currency for another. Considered safe places to keep money because they were protected by the gods, temples accumulated enormous sums not only given as offerings but held in trust. The banking enterprise thus came to center about places of worship. As Neill Hamilton describes it, the "security factor attracted the surplus funds of states, corporations, and private individuals until custody of deposits became a regular feature of temples. . . . In addition to currency exchange, deposits, and loans temple banks could arrange transfer of funds from one part of the ancient world to another." [3] From references in Second Maccabees,[4] it is clear that the Jerusalem Temple, like other temples throughout the Hellenistic world, contained a bank. Under the umbrella of divine protection, the financial services proliferated. Temple personnel included custodians of all sorts, secretaries and accountants to record loans, and purchasing agents and paymasters engaged in the enormous effort to rebuild and maintain the edifice and its auxiliary structures. As a result, the Temple treasury in Jerusalem

> played the part of a state exchequer, which was otherwise lacking in Judaea. . . . [The] priests who stood at the head of the cult also held the secular power. . . . [The] majority of the owners of the deposits belonged to the same limited circle of Jerusalem aristocracy of which the governing priesthood were also members. If an owner of capital could place his means in the Temple treasury on deposit, why should he not also obtain from it sums of money in the form of loans? [5]

The ramifications of this reached beyond the Temple; the interlocking system affected the construction of walls, towers, aqueducts, and other projects throughout the area. Student scholarships were offered to encourage Torah study. Wine, oil, and flour, purchased from the surplus in the Shekel-chamber, were resold to pilgrims bringing private offerings, the profits falling to the Temple. In the Court of the Gentiles the sale of sacrificial animals prospered. For the Passover in A.D. 66 alone, the number of lambs slaughtered is estimated to have been 255,600. Thus the Temple establishment was in actuality "the royal bank of Judea," representing an investment which the Sadducees closely guarded. They would fight rather than switch, as any budding messiah soon discovered, the Sadducees promptly turning him over to the Roman authorities as a potential insurrectionist.

The Romans, for their part, brooked no interference with law and order. During the year a garrison manned the Fortress Antonia overlooking the Temple precincts; and for the Passover festival, Pontius Pilate arrived from Caesarea on the coast with reinforcements to take personal command. While the government of Judea rested in the hands of the Sadducees led by the High Priest, Pilate was still responsible to his superiors in Rome should a civil disturbance break out. Pilate is pictured in the Gospels as vacillating and weak willed, and by the Jews (à la Flavius Josephus) as tyrannical, corrupt, and cruel. But one wonders how Pilate managed to last ten years as governor of Judea if such was his nature. Presented with an excitable people whose customs he could not appreciate and whose leadership was quick to exploit any sign of weakness in him, Pilate was in all probability typical of most officials the emperor relied upon: loyal, tough, strict, and competent. The power of his office was there to be used, and Pilate would have used it.

Faced with implacable foes, therefore, Jesus arrived in the Jerusalem area under the most unfavorable circumstances. What possessed Him to think he could reverse the currents of accommodation there? The ruling clique showed no desire for the righteousness He demanded; their "righteousness" was perfunctory, skin thin. The scholars of proud rabbinical schools would also reject His apocalyptic summons. What did Jesus hope to accomplish?

Perhaps He hoped for a miracle. The purging of Judea's pure and "separated ones" with spiritual fire, the mighty infusion of others with the same Spirit which commanded Him—that would be a miracle!

In all honesty, though, it must be confessed we do not know how Jesus conceived of Himself or what He anticipated doing. Not only the description of His Passion but that of events immediately before is so influenced by religious trauma and doctrinal considerations as to make this impossible in any absolute sense. Early Christians could not and did not attempt to distinguish between the actual fact of Jesus' death and their emotional response to it. They viewed His Passion through eyes of faith. The spiritual dimensions they saw there they pictured in the language of fidelity and love. With the Apostles they then declared:

> We must obey God rather than men. The God of our fathers raised Jesus whom you killed by hanging him on a tree. God exalted him at his right hand as Leader and Savior, to give repentance to Israel and forgiveness of sins. And we are witnesses to these things.
> (Acts 5:29–32)

In the afterglow of any spiritual titan, the adulation of admirers soon begins to recast the record of failures and achievements. Thus, unaided by authenticated letters and sound motion picture coverage, historians must strain reality from an ocean of half-truth, hearsay, and sincere but misled assumptions. Allowance must be made for the disparagement of skeptics and foes that followers of a slain leader will wish to mitigate. The circumstances surrounding the assassination of Abraham Lincoln, for instance, are by no means clear,[6] and this but a century after a killing which happened when camera and news reporters were active! How understandable, then, are the debates as to Jesus' motives as He shifted His attention to Jerusalem. Did He conceive of Himself as personally fulfilling the role of Israel prophesied by Isaiah?

> He was despised and rejected by men;
>   a man of sorrows, and acquainted with grief. . . .
> Surely he has borne our griefs
>   and carried our sorrows;
> yet we esteemed him stricken,
>   smitten by God, and afflicted.
> But he was wounded for our transgressions,
>   he was bruised for our iniquities;
> upon him was the chastisement that made us
>   whole,
>   and with his stripes we are healed.
> (Isa. 53:3–5)

Members of the primitive Christian fellowship saw in Jesus a suffering redeemer who came to serve and give His life a ransom for many.[7] But did Jesus so see Himself? An indisputable answer to this evades us.

The church acclaimed Jesus as a spiritual rather than military Messiah. But did Jesus see Himself in that framework of reference? Again we are left uncertain.

First-generation Christians identified their risen Lord with the "Son of Man," that other-worldly image of apocalyptic hope. Did Jesus so identify Himself—and, if so, to what extent? Again—unresolved questions.

Since no final reconstruction of the Jerusalem ministry is possible, we shall not attempt it. Rather, we shall begin where Mark did: with two facts so consistently affirmed as to appear irrefutable. The two facts are that at Jerusalem Jesus was crucified by the Romans, and that afterward He appeared to His disciples. Beginning with this, then, we shall sketch in what must remain an approximation of events during the final period of Jesus' life.

Let it be noted at the outset that the Gospel of Mark is stylistically crude. This is not a modern but ancient verdict, Hippolytus judging Mark clumsy in writing ("stub-fingered").[8] In all probability, when the more polished Gospel of Matthew appeared, it was eagerly read as much superior with its enlarged and improved discourses, so that the version by Mark soon fell into disuse.

The Gospel of Mark nevertheless represents the first attempt to preserve the story of Jesus in written form.[9] The occasion was the sudden martyrdom of Peter in Rome about A.D. 64–67. There in the Imperial City the now aged apostle addressed the Greek-speaking congregation in his native Aramaic by means of interpreters. From all indications one of these interpreters was Mark, who evidently wrote down afterward what he recalled of Peter's preaching.

Then, suddenly, Peter was crucified, his voice forever stilled, his reminiscences grown now more priceless. At once the need to preserve what he had said was felt. How had Jesus the

Messiah lived and died? How had God raised Him from the dead to glory whence He soon would return to judge the world and establish the Kingdom? Mark determined to save what he could of the apostolic message. Because it was uppermost in his readers' minds and, next to the Resurrection, closest in time, Mark began with the Passion story. Working backward in sequence by means of what information he and others possessed, he proceeded to sort out and fit together bits of treasured memory into as convincing a narrative as possible.

It was not easy. Almost at once, Mark found himself in difficulty: so much of Jesus' time in Jerusalem had been left unaccounted for in the tradition passed down. Surely Jesus and His disciples had done and said more. But what? No record existed. Mark, therefore, did as necessity directed. He reduced the length of Jesus' stay in Jerusalem to a minimum and then filled the empty hours with selected episodes and discourses. Between the Temple Cleansing and Last Supper he sandwiched four pieces of tradition which already had been to some degree influenced by Christian persecution and privation: the Little Apocalypse (chapter 13), the legend of the barren fig tree (Israel) that withered under Jesus' curse (Mark 11:12–14, 20–21), the annointing of Jesus at the house of Simon the leper (Mark 14:3–9),[10] and the parable of the wicked husbandmen who slew the rightful heir to a vineyard (Mark 12:1–11).

Other material was inserted for different reasons. Desiring to present Jesus as a spiritual Messiah who remained aloof from revolutionary politics, Mark includes a confrontation over the lawfulness of paying tribute (12:13–17). Some readers might wonder if Jesus was always controversial in His teaching, and so Mark adds—immediately after some criticism of scribes— the commendation of a poor widow who contributed sacrificially to the Temple treasury while the rich gave merely "out of their abundance" (12:41–44). The fact that Jesus held His own under examination, despite a lack of scribal training, is important to Mark; Jesus is thus seen answering without hesitation or embarrassment questions concerning His authority (11:27–33), the resurrection of the dead (12:18–27), and the greatest commandment (12:28–34). The selection and placement of this material is quite arbitrary. Mark is not writing a history so much as an interpretation of his Lord in the light of a victorious faith. The result is a narrative in which unrealistic shifts in action occur. For instance, when Jesus reaches the Temple following a tumultuous entrance to the city, the cheering of the crowd abruptly stops (11:11). Jesus looks around "at everything" and leaves. The next morning He is back, but no one seems to recall the demonstration of the previous afternoon. Cleansing the Temple, Jesus again leaves only to be discovered later sitting quietly and unaccosted opposite the Temple treasury. The feeling of improbability about this is simply the consequence of an effort to reconcile irreconcilable pieces of tradition.

With this discussion behind us, we can turn now to examine those happenings which most excited Christian devotion: the Triumphant Entry and Temple Cleansing, the Last Supper, the Garden Agony, and the Passion. Initially the terse narrative appears on the surface question-free, but questions do pose themselves upon closer examination. Was the dramatic entrance of Jesus deliberately staged by Him as Mark maintains, or was it a spontaneous occurrence which later the Church concluded could not have happened unplanned? Did the Triumphant Entry occur as described, or is Mark recording an invented incident born of Christian devotion, which could not believe that Jesus the Messiah would enter Jerusalem other than amid open acclaim? Were Roman Christians in particular attracted to this picture of their Lord as a conquering hero because it resembled the periodic return of victorious generals of Rome riding in chariots preceded by trumpets and drums and followed by marching legions?

Another question relates to the continued freedom of Jesus despite His disruptive acts. Why was not Jesus apprehended

at once by the Jerusalem police—or, if they failed, by the
Romans? Is it not unreasonable to believe that the authorities
would allow a Galilean prophet to *ride* into Jerusalem on the
threshold of a patriotic festival, and do this amid throngs of
ecstatic pilgrims who could not fail to recognize in His riding
a claim to regal power? When Jesus chased the money-changers
and salesmen out of the Temple, why did not the Temple police
or, the Roman troops stationed nearby arrest Him? This is
puzzling, especially when Mark indicates that Jesus lingered
in the vicinity after the uproar. The only explanation offered
is that the chief priests and scribes heard about the demonstration but were afraid to arrest Jesus because "the multitude was
astonished at his teaching" (Mark 11:18). This seems a lame
excuse when one considers how quickly security forces in Jerusalem responded to the later preaching of Peter, Stephen, and
Paul (Acts 4:3; 5:17, 26; 6:12; 21:30–33).

In answer, it appears to me that certain conclusions are unavoidable. The first is that Christians came early to think of the
Triumphant Entry and Temple Cleansing as closely related and
part of a divine demonstration of Jesus kingship. Both actions
—the riding into a city and the challenging of a Temple bank—
were royal prerogatives. Their character was such that no Jew
or Gentile could miss their significance. Lest the claim be
missed, however, the fulfillment of Messianic prophecy is implied:

> Rejoice greatly, O daughter of Zion!
>   Shout aloud, O daughter of Jerusalem!
> Lo, your king comes to you;
>   triumphant and victorious is he,
> humble and riding on an ass,
>   on the colt the foal of an ass.
> I will cut off the chariot from Ephraim
>   and the war horse from Jerusalem;
> and the battle bow shall be cut off,
>   and he shall command peace to the nations;

his dominion shall be from sea to sea,
    and from the River to the ends of the earth.[11]
(Zech. 9:9–10)

It must be remembered that the tradition we have in Mark arose out of the Church which, at its inception, was a movement of shattered Messianic hopes, a movement which projected Messianic claims backward upon its slain Lord to meet its needs of faith. Behind the Entry and Cleansing, therefore, may well lie a kernel of solid fact, but what actually happened has been so embellished with retelling and veneered by religious expectation as to be no longer discernible.

Another conclusion is that Mark has telescoped what was a longer ministry in Jerusalem. As in the case of Jesus' sojourns in Gentile territory, Mark has shortened considerably an itinerary of which he has little knowledge. While he offers some evidence of a teaching ministry, the primary concern of Mark in connection with Jerusalem is the Passion story.

One scholar who theorizes that Jesus stayed in Jerusalem a longer period is Maurice Goguel.[12] He believes that if one follows the chronology of the Fourth Gospel (which does not labor under the imposed doctrine of Jesus as the suffering Messiah) one finds Jesus entering Jerusalem not a few days before the Passover but at the Feast of Tabernacles, in either September or October. In Jerusalem Jesus remains until the Feast of the Dedication in December. He then retires to the district of Perea across the Jordan. When He returns to the city, it is but six days before the Passover (John 12:1), or about the time set by Matthew, Mark, and Luke. The fact that the latter three Gospels have reduced the stay in Jerusalem almost to a minimum, says Goguel, "is due, doubtless, to the fact that they have confused the arrival of Jesus at Jerusalem with his return to the city." [13]

The picture of the activity of Jesus at Jerusalem has been perverted in the Synoptic narratives, partly under the influence of the idea that Jesus only went up to Jerusalem to die and partly owing to the confusion by which Mark has reduced the length of the stay of Jesus in Jerusalem to a few days; this prevented him from conceiving the idea of an actual ministry of preaching, and led him to regard the time in Jerusalem simply as a period of preparation for the Passion.[14]

Many scholars of course disagree, favoring the chronology of events given in the synoptics. But there is no denying that the Johannine chronology resolves a number of questions, or that others besides Goguel feel the Fourth Gospel more accurate at this point.[15] Something like a "triumphant entry" could have occurred if a prophet had preached before in the area. The cheers of a crowd would then be understandable. Similarly, a realistic pattern of hostility falls into place, the astonishment of the authorities turning gradually into fear and finally murderous resentment.[16] In the Gospel of John, the cleansing of the Temple is set well in advance of the final Passover (2:13–20), and the protest of Jesus is directed against irreverent trading in the Court of the Gentiles rather than, as the synoptics imply, against the perversion of a spiritual purpose through converting the Temple into "a den of robbers" (Matt. 21:13, Mark 11:17; Luke 19:46). The suspicion grows, therefore, that in Mark (and subsequently Matthew and Luke) the Temple Cleansing has been placed after the Triumphant Entry because there is nowhere else to locate it, Jesus having traveled—according to these Gospels—only once to Jerusalem during His mission. If this is true, then the tie between the "Cleansing" and the Passover feast is by no means unassailable. Not only the first three Gospels but the Fourth Gospel as well (2:13) may be seen as merely conforming to a deeply set but erroneous assumption. The disruptive act might just as easily have occurred at another time when Temple and Roman guards would have been less alert and reinforced, thus making the escape of Jesus more explicable.

The Last Supper has long raised questions. When exactly

did it take place? Was it an ordinary supper held just before the festival, or was it actually the Passover meal on the end of which Jesus attached a special rite? The confusion comes about because Mark offers two dates for the Last Supper. He introduces the annointing scene at the home of Simon the leper with with the observation, "It was now two days before the Passover and the feast of Unleavened Bread" (14:1), and then almost at once describes the preparations for the Supper, beginning with "And on the first day of Unleavened Bread, when they sacrificed the passover lamb" (14:12).

Why the contradiction? The reason would seem to be that Mark had on hand two traditions and, not wishing to discard either, he used both. Mark, however, does distinguish between them by placing one more prominently. Set in opposing columns, the characteristics of these Passover traditions compare as follows:

14:1, 17–25	*14:12–16, 26–30*
prominent position	somewhat subordinate
primitive origin	later origin
concerns eating of meal	concerns meal preparation
Paschal lamb unmentioned	Paschal lamb mentioned
death of Jesus *before* the Passover	death *after* the Passover
length of Jesus' stay in Jerusalem uncertain	length of stay one week (probably influenced by Holy Week tradition)
	hymn *(Hallel)* sung and denial by Peter predicted

This would lead us to believe that Jesus probably did not live to eat the Passover with His disciples. He ate instead an ordinary meal at the close of which He used a broken loaf and common cup to prophesy His imminent death and signify His voluntary acceptance of it. To what degree the Eucharist came to affect the later memory of this final meal is unclear, but there is little doubt that the description given in Mark, though more primitive than Paul's (1 Cor. 11:23–26), is intended to establish the origin of the Church rite and determine the manner in which it should be observed.

Lastly, we come to the Passion story. Arranged for maximum effect, the account of Jesus' arrest, trial, and execution is designed to win converts and to strengthen the faith of those already committed. Judged in the light of this aim, the narration in every respect is masterful. Not even Plato's description of the death of Socrates compares in pathos with that of Jesus.

For this reason the Passion Story must be accepted for what it is: *history subjectively interpreted.* This applies to all the Gospels. Each is an apostolic instrument for preaching the saving message of God in Jesus Christ. Each in its own way endeavors to convince the doubter, rebuke the wayward, and exhort the faithful. The Passion story is thus preeminently a document of faith.

This faith perspective the historian must respect. He certainly cannot ignore it. In Mark's account of the Passion, one senses at once the need to explain the death of Jesus. Quite unlike present-day Christians, the first Christians were untroubled by how Jesus rose from the dead but very troubled as to why He died in the first place, and by means of one of the most abominable tortures ever devised. In reply, Mark explains by means of his Gospel that Jesus perished because He went to Jerusalem where envious Jewish leaders rejected His message and handed Him over to the Romans. All this was, of course, that Scripture might be fulfilled in compliance with the will of God.

Hence in the Gospels, beginning with Mark, some scenes have obviously been protracted and detailed for added emphasis. The Trial, in comparison with the Crucifixion, is described at length because it fixes the blame for Jesus' death irrevocably upon the Jews. Pilate, meanwhile, is cast more favorably: " 'Why, what evil has he done?' But they shouted all the more, 'Crucify him.' So Pilate, wishing to satisfy the crowd, released for them Barabbas; and having scourged Jesus, he delivered him to be crucified" (Mark 15:14–15). In short, Pilate agreed to the execution only under extreme pressure. It is to be noted furthermore that while the henchmen of the High Priest manhandle Jesus before His conviction (Mark 14:65), the Romans mock and scourge Him only after his guilt has been established and sentence passed (Mark 15:16–20). When Jesus on the Cross breathes His last, it is significantly a Roman officer who declares, "Truly this man was a son of God!" (Mark 15:39), a judgment in which all the guards are made to join in the Gospel of Matthew (27:54). By the time Luke's Gospel made its appearance, the need to erase forever any trace of sedition had grown still more imperative. The opinion of Pilate—"I have found in him no crime deserving death" (Luke 23:22)—is therefore repeated by another Roman, this time at the Cross: "Certainly this man was innocent!" (Luke 23:47).

In contrast to the Trial, which substantiates the guilt of the Jews and the Roman opinion that Jesus was innocent, other segments of the Passion are treated with deliberate restraint. Mark states that Jesus arrived at Gethsemane "greatly distressed and troubled" (14:33), a diagnosis which in the Greek text denotes heavy emotional shock.[17] Matthew at this juncture (26:37) dilutes the "greatly distressed" to a rather tame "sorrowful." It may be but an instance of literary polishing and, again, it may be more. The fact that Luke omits entirely any reference to Jesus' distraught condition makes one feel the fact was embarrassing to early Christians.

Equally embarrassing was the cowardly flight of the disciples when their Master was arrested. Once more Mark makes scant mention of it; Matthew, unable to expunge it, lets the single reference stand; but Luke drops from his Gospel even that (Mark 14:50; Matt. 26:56). For this and other reasons, the preceding action of resistance with swords (Mark 14:47; Matt. 26:51–52; Luke 22:49–51) may be considered historically doubtful. An ascending elaboration in Matthew and Luke is obvious. Also of doubtful historicity is the story of Peter's going to the house of High Priest where, accosted, he denies knowing Jesus (Mark

14:54, 66–72; Matt. 26:58, 69–75; Luke 22:54–62). After the Resurrection, Christians inevitably wanted to know why the disciples did nothing to save Jesus from the mob. The question must have haunted those who ran. The need for a defense became urgent therefore, particularly since Peter and the others were now esteemed Apostles. So the tradition, once sown, took eager root: the disciples had indeed resisted the arrest; they had fled only when told by their Master that fulfillment of prophecy dictated flight; Peter had actually followed the mob at great risk and penetrated the High Priest's courtyard, and surely would have done more had not the prediction of Jesus and the will of God been fulfilled in a panic-stricken denial. In this manner the cowardice of Peter was made palatable and his escape explained despite his followng Jesus into the very stronghold of the enemy.

We can guess, though, that there was another reason this story became firmly rooted. It was comforting. The Church in Italy and throughout Asia Minor was experiencing repeated outbreaks of persecution. Nero's blood-bath in A.D. 64 was a horror, but no less terrifying were local persecutions which occurred here and there, leaving Christians nervous as to where the next cry would be sounded against them. Recalling the story of Peter's shame, how proud some Christians must have been to have withstood testing. Others who, under threat of death, renounced their faith would have found in the story the courage to rejoin their congregation. So a growing tradition that silenced awkward questions served to stiffen Christian resolve as well.

As for the actual execution, the details stand out in clean, hard lines like a stone relief, the ghoulish scene reclothed in the robes of tragic heroism. With their theme of a suffering redeemer, how remarkable it is that the Gospels do not linger over gruesome details as do later descriptions.

> Nothing could be more horrible than the sight of this living body, breathing, seeing, hearing, still able to feel, and yet

reduced to the state of a corpse by forced immobility and
absolute helplessness. We cannot even say that the crucified
person writhed in agony, for it was impossible for him to
move . . . to brush away the flies.[18]

This we are spared by the Gospels. The sight of crucified slaves
and renegades was so familiar that the picture sprang naturally
to the minds of readers—the slow, labored procession . . . the
drugged wine . . . the division of clothing . . . the mockery . . .
the cry of dereliction . . . the final collapse of flesh and will.
Once freed of expressions of later Christian apology and adoration,[19] the narrative reveals how ordinary was the death of Jesus.
Under a tropic sun He died, His Crucifixion no different from
thousands of others that further brutalized an already brutal age.

The death of Jesus left His disciples aghast with dismay and
grief. Nothing could be more understandable now as we seek
to relive in present tense what may have happened . . .

For months the disciples travel with Jesus, catch His enthusiasm, share His faith. When the time comes to depart for Jerusalem, they accompany Him out of genuine love and respect.

Arriving several months before the Passover, Jesus frequents
the Temple, preaching with increased effectiveness. As before in
Galilee, His audience swells with each passing day until many
come early to hear Him and stay late. The sick are also brought,
and healings occur under the inspiration of the moment.

Once again, however, a familiar pattern of opposition exhibits itself. The popularity of Jesus ignites rabbinical jealousy,
the force of His unlettered humanity being taken as arrogance
by stiff scholars. The Sadducees, too, are threatened by His
influence over the people and conclude that He must be politically ambitious. Finally some incident brings matters to a head
(possibly just such an incident as a "cleansing"). The greediness
of money-changers and salesmen, the bawling and bleating of
animals is more than Jesus' religious sensibilities can bear. It is
as if their presence in the Temple symbolizes the perversion of

everything that is sacred and elevating and, in a rage, He drives out the offending tradesmen and beasts. So unexpected is His act that the Temple guards fail to apprehend him.

Slipping away from the city, Jesus retreats to Perea across the Jordan, there biding His time in seclusion until the Passover. He then reenters Jerusalem amid excited crowds arriving for the festival. A number of pilgrims recognize Him, as do city dwellers, and welcoming cheers break out. In the jostling throng, however, the effect of His entrance is swallowed up and largely lost, so that when Jesus enters the Temple He is unsuccessful in moving its elite with his message. Nor does the populace rise in a spontaneous demand for national repentance and revival. Jesus therefore leaves soon after.

This time, though, His enemies are ready. Pilate has been informed of the troublemaker's return, and arrangements are made by the Temple aristocracy for His arrest.

Aware that a hostile ring is closing about Him, Jesus nevertheless slips back into Jerusalem with His disciples under cover of night for a final meal. Afterwards, in a grove of trees outside the city, a posse bursts upon the group and seizes Jesus. His followers panic and run, their sole thought being escape.

Morning finds Jesus before the Sanhedrin. The accusation is clear, the questioning brief, the decision predictable. Jesus is passed along to Pilate. Another hearing, the expected verdict, and within a short time Jesus is crucified. Death comes surprisingly fast, but not fast enough to numb the acute sense of spiritual desertion He feels.

"My God, my God, why hast thou forsaken me?"

NOTES

1. *First prediction:* Matt. 16:13–23; Mark 8:27–33; Luke 9:18–22. *Second prediction:* Matt. 17:22–23; Mark 9:30–32; Luke 9:43–45. *Third prediction:* Matt. 20:17–19; Mark 10:32–34; Luke 18:31–34.

2. Here I accept the scholarship of those who, like Morton S. Enslin, contest the traditionally held view that Jesus' audience dwindled away in Galilee until He and the Twelve were left virtually alone when the end came. Dr. Enslin's position appears reasonable and sound when he says, "Had not Jesus' companions become convinced—perhaps more deeply than some of them at the moment realized—of the rightness of his claim to be a prophet sent by God, it is highly improbable that they would have seen him on Easter morning. It was the deathless confidence he had roused in his hearers that by the power of God he had spoken as 'no other man spake' which led to their passionate belief that he must have triumphed over death and was still alive" (*The Prophet from Nazareth,* p. 91). The thesis of Ernst Lohmeyer that a strong following of Jesus continued in Galilee after the Resurrection would support this (see footnote 10, Chapter 4).

3. N. Q. Hamilton, "Temple Cleansing and Temple Bank," *Journal of Biblical Literature* 83, Part 4 (1964), pp. 365–72. The sentences quoted are from page 366 of that source.

4. "And reported that the treasury in Jerusalem was full of such untold quantities of money that the amount of the funds was beyond computation; and that they did not belong to the account of the sacrifices and they might fall under the control of the king" (2 Macc. 3:6. Smith-Goodspeed translation, Chicago: University of Chicago, 1939).

"The high priest pointed out that some deposits belonged to widows and orphans, and one belonged to Hyrcanus, son of Tobias, a man of very high position— . . . that it all amounted to four hundred talents of silver and two hundred of gold, and that it was absolutely impossible that those who were relying on the sacredness of the place and on the sanctity and inviolability of the temple, which was repected all over the world, should be wronged" (2 Macc. 3:10–12. Smith-Goodspeed translation).

5. V. Tcherikover, *Hellenistic Civilization and the Jews,* (Philadelphia: The Jewish Publication Society of America, 1959), pp. 155–56.

6. The confusing aspects of the Lincoln murder are fully described in Theodore Roscoe's *Web of Conspiracy* (Englewood Cliffs, N. J.: Prentice-Hall, Inc. 1959).

7. Matt. 20:28, Mark 10:45, I Tim. 2:5–6; see also Luke 24:25–27, Acts 8:27–35.

8. Hippolytus, *Refutation* vii. 18. See: Hippolytus, *Philosophumena, or, the Refutation of All Heresies: Formerly Attributed to Ongen, but Not to Hippolytus, Bishop and Martyr.* rev. ed. Legge, F., tr. New York: Ktav Publishing House, 1972.

9. More than one theory exists as to how the Gospel of Mark originated. Edgar J. Goodspeed (see *An Introduction to the New Testament,* Chicago, University of Chicago Press, 1937, Chapter 10) represents the traditional view that John Mark wrote down the Apostle Peter's fresh and vivid memories of Jesus, and then organized them into a pamphlet-gospel soon after Peter's martyrdom. This is the general position I have taken, but the reader should be equally aware of the "Multiple Source Hypothesis" expounded by Frederick C. Grant more recently (see *The Earliest Gospel,* Nashville: Abingdon Press, 1943, Chapter 2 and 3) which replaces the exclusive testimony of one man "with the 'social' tradition of a whole community, the widely shared possession of a whole group—of two groups, in fact, the Palestinian and the Roman" (p. 73). According to the Grant hypothesis, "the 'development' of the Gospel *in its author's own mind* was perhaps as follows" (p. 71). The Passion story came first and was prefaced with controversies with Jewish authorities. Next the Petrine element was added, chiefly at the beginning of the narrative. To give samples of Jesus' teaching, the author then inserted passages from "Q" or some other collection of oral tradition. The "Little Apocalypse" came next to answer pressing questions arising in the Church at Rome at that time. Finally, an additional "mass of current *oral tradition*—not so extensive in Rome, probably, as in Palestine and Syria—was drawn upon for additional material upon numerous points as the narrative proceeded" (p. 71).

10. While Matthew copies this incident in his Gospel (26:6–13), Luke locates it much earlier in the ministry of Jesus at the house of a Pharisee in Galilee (7:36–38). John, on the other hand, situates it the day before the triumphal entry (12:1–8).

11. Reflected in Mark 11:2–7, and quoted in part in Matt. 21:4–5.

12. M. Goguel, *Jesus and the Origins of Christianity,* vol. 2, Chapters 8 and 14.

13. Ibid., p. 400.

14. Ibid., p. 405.

15. See W. F. Howard's arguments in favor of the Johannine placement of the Temple cleansing much earlier in the ministry of Jesus (*The Interpreter's Bible,* vol. 8, pp. 447–48).

16. Maurice Goguel views the break as coming at the point where the enemies of Jesus resolve to find out definitely where He stands. Is He or is He not the promised Messiah (for that is the intent behind their questions)? His reply causes a final, irreparable break in relations:

"And they tried to arrest him, but feared the multitude." See M. Goguel, *Jesus and the Origins of Christianity,* p. 423.

17. The Greek present infinitive of ἐκθαμβέω (ekthāmbeō) rendered in the Revised Standard Version as "greatly distressed and troubled" Mark 14:33) means literally "to be amazed or awe-struck." On the face of it, this is strange and makes little sense. One plausible explanation is that Jesus was not amazed at all. He only looked amazed—his mouth dropping open, His eyes wide and staring. Actually He was in deep shock.

18. Albert Réville, *Jésus de Nazareth,* trans. M. Goguel (Paris: Librairie Fischbacher, 1906), p. 370.

19. These elements, imposed on the Crucifixion by later religious devotion, may be promptly identified. Inasmuch as the disciples had fled, women—including Mary, the mother of Jesus—are said to have witnessed the death from a distance (Mark 15:40–41; Matt. 27:55–56; Luke 23:49). While followers of Jesus might have watched "from afar," the reference gives every impression of being tacked on in order to guarantee, by the presence of the women, the truth of details already given and those soon to be added (note particularly "all his acquaintances and the women . . . saw these things"—Luke 23:49).

Other instances of accretion are the scorning of Christ (Mark 15:31–32; Matt. 27:42–43; Luke 23:35), the supernatural darkness (Mark 15:33; Matt. 27:45; Luke 23:44), the rending of the curtain in the Holy of Holies (Mark 15:38; Matt. 27:51; Luke 23:45), the affirmation of the Centurion (Mark 15:39; Matt. 27:54; Luke 23:47). Matthew goes the farthest in his elaboration: *all* the Roman guards acclaim Jesus (Matt. 27:54), and at the moment of His death the earth shakes, rocks split, tombs are opened, "many bodies of the saints" who have died are raised, and coming out of the tombs "after his [Jesus'] resurrection" they go into the holy city and appear to many there (Matt. 27:51–53). Such implanted post-Resurrection material is undisguised and easily recognized.

Epilogue

As I type this closing word, I am impressed by the similarity in atmosphere that exists between the first century and our own. Terrorism, kidnappings, and "royal scandals" have merely donned modern dress. Political assassination and economic oppression still scar human existence deeply, as do the scourges of hunger, poverty, ignorance, and disease.

The first century Zealot, Pharisee, Sadducee, Essene, and Herodian pressed his particular solution to the quandary in which Jews found themselves. Today, in our nation, different political and social groups compete for voters' support, and who can predict what new voices will surface tomorrow? All the while, drop-outs wander the land, and pseudo-religious communes divorce themselves from society they believe too sick to recover. In this respect how little has changed since Jesus emerged from Nazareth to summon men to a creative revolution.

It is equally clear that Christians in this period of blistering change must both recognize and *accept* the true character of Jesus as one who shook His listeners to their roots. Much in the Church today unfortunately denies the revolutionary stance of its Lord, the prevailing congregational mood being that of bland worship in place of forthright, even controversial action. Yet Jesus was a prophet, not a priest; an activist, not a spectator. His gift was a venturesome life style founded upon an undivided loyalty to God. Thus if the Church is to follow Him, it must now move forward as a pilgrim people with fresh enlightenment and concern. Experimentation through new forms of ministry is called for, the risks of active involvement being accepted and with them the consequence of possible failure.

It was the inspiration of that One Uncompromising Life which stirred such influential Christians as Toyohiko Kagawa, the gentle-spirited social reformer and evangelist, and Dietrich Bonhoeffer, whose book, *The Cost of Discipleship,* was illustrated by his death on a Nazi gallows. More recently the same inspiration of the Spirit has glowed in the warning of Halford Luccock that "if the church marries a given generation, she is sure to be a widow in the next, and that without visible means of support." And the rebuke of Harry Emerson Fosdick that "Christians are supposed not merely to endure change, nor even to profit by it, but to cause it." And the spur provided by Roger Hazelton that "The Church and its ministry . . . exist wherever Christians have hard choices to make, hostility to face, misunderstanding to overcome, despair to struggle with, doubts to resolve." [1]

Beyond this I would say that in Jesus of Nazareth there resides a certain inexhaustibility. I do not know what else to call this feeling which grows as one journeys ever deeper into the Gospel documents. The opinion of W. B. Sutphin [2] that Jesus cannot be compressed in creeds or locked between bookends but affirms this sensation. One might as well try to experience the magnitude of the ocean in a thimbleful of salt water as to think one can offer the last word about Jesus. It is not the lack of any "diary" of Jesus but the awesomeness of His moral character and spiritual amplitude that defies a neat, final packaging. When, therefore, Mark records the announcement to the women at the empty tomb, he expresses an enduring truth about Jesus:

> "Do not be amazed:
> you seek Jesus of Nazareth,
> who was crucified.

He has risen, he is not here;
    see the place where they laid
    him.
But go, tell his disciples and
    Peter that he is going before
    you to Galilee.
(16:5–7)

Such is the way of Jesus. He is forever out on the road ahead of us who so timidly follow.

This leads us to close with a look at the Resurrection event itself. No study of Jesus can properly ignore it. That act of God so exalted Jesus in the hearts and minds of His disciples as to make it impossible for them to reflect upon His life and death apart from what ensued, or His Resurrection apart from what preceded. The Crucifixion-Resurrection event was one and indivisible. "He who was" soon became "He who is," so that when Paul wrote the Philippians he could pray in one breath that he might know Christ and the power of His Resurrection, and in the next that he might share in Christ's sufferings, "becoming like him in his death" (Phil. 3:11).

That the Resurrection was a certainty for the disciples is clear. The earliest record, which Paul provides, never wavers in its belief that Jesus reappeared to those who loved and obeyed Him: "He appeared to Cephas, then to the twelve . . . to more than five hundred brethren at one time . . . to James, then to the apostles. Last of all, as to one untimely born, he appeared also to me. (1 Cor. 15:5–8). Analytical psychology has been applied to this phenomenon and various theories offered, but in the end the Resurrection stands in a class by itself. John Knox, it seems to me, comes closest to explaining the unexplainable when he submits that "the primitive Christian community was not a memorial society with its eyes fastened on a departed master; it was a dynamic community created around a living and present Lord." This living memory residing in the community of believers is, to his mind, one of the most profound meanings of the Resurrection:

> This means, not a memory, however sharp and vivid, in the minds and hearts of individual disciples, but rather a shared remembrance, alive and growing, and not less true, but rather more deeply true, on that account. Papias at the middle of the second century speaks of it as "the living voice"; that voice began to speak from the moment of the Resurrection, and it speaks still. This memory of Jesus has its unique character because it is memory, not of one who was, but of one who is. The one who is remembered is still known; the one who is known is also remembered.[3]

This "living voice" was the bedrock experience upon which the Church coalesced. It is still the touchstone of religious faith by which Christians affirm, "The Lord is risen indeed!" Thus the Easter narratives—women at the Tomb, disciples in the Upper Room, sorrowing travelers on the Emmaus Road, weary fishermen on the Sea of Tiberias—all clothe as best the human tongue can a shared experience which must have been incredibly convincing. How else are we to explain the obvious change in those who first gathered as the Church, who emerged from hiding to preach openly in the name of their crucified Lord, who with audacity abandoned the Jewish Sabbath as their day of worship in favor of the first day of the week, when their Lord rose?

Words do not readily capture an experience of such magnitude. We have pictured Jesus as carrying on His mission in the face of a mounting storm that broke in Jerusalem. If this is an accurate representation (and I believe it is), then the Resurrection experience most likely burst upon the disciples in Galilee much like sunshine through clouds after a violent electrical storm.

I recall such a moment of serene delight following a storm in Ohio. I was fifteen then and working with an uncle during the haying season. That July on the farm had been a breathless march of drought-laden days, and so it was with mixed feelings that we sensed in the heavy air, the biting insects and the silent birds the approach of a storm, Finally, in the west, the sky turned to ink and a low growl of thunder reached us. No sooner had we driven the team and wagon into the barn than a milk-white curtain of rain uncoiled its full length and raced toward us. Overhead the tin roof roared as thousands of watery fists pounded it; barn doors rattled in the wind; a loaded apple tree thrashed back and forth and then split in two; and twilight fell in a fog of torrential rain. Only shafts of periodic lightning penetrated the gloom. The unleashed fury was enough to paralyze the mind.

Then, almost as suddenly as it came, the storm fled, the downpour slackening to a sprinkle and then dying altogether. Save for the leftover dripping of water from the eaves and a gushing sound in the spouting, there was silence. In the unexpected calm, the earth seemed to hold its breath lest the battle resume.

Sliding back the barn door, I stepped out and looked around. As I did, sunlight burst through, and in that instant the world was reborn and me with it. How clean and cool the air felt after weeks of humidity and dust. Sounds, unnoticed before, came with startling clarity—the crowing of a bantam rooster, the lowing of a cow, the twittering of sparrows splashing in a puddle.

And the sun! Its brilliance lighted the heavens and earth as if in benediction. The grass was greener, the sky bluer. And in the distance, arching over all, a rainbow more vivid than any I could remember.

As I relive the ecstasy of that moment, I am confident the disciples experienced emotionally no less exhilaration and certainly more at the reappearance of their Lord. In the Resurrection, His presence broke upon them like dazzling sunlight. He whom they mourned as lost was recognized. They felt pulsing through their fellowship the same Spirit which animated Him;

in its power they saw Him and rejoiced. The purposes of God He embodied had not been thwarted; instead His spiritual vitality, freed of corporeal limitations, became magnified many times over. Each Lord's Day, in the breaking of the bread, He made Himself known and their hearts burned within them (Luke 24:28–35). The kingdom He proclaimed grew more real, more imminent.

With what fearless certainty, therefore, Peter and the other Apostles could preach a reality beyond doubt:

> Men of Israel, hear these words:
> Jesus of Nazareth,
> a man attested to you by God
> with mighty works and wonders
> and signs which God did through him
> in your midst, as you yourselves know—
> this Jesus,
> delivered up according to the definite plan
> and foreknowledge of God,
> you crucified and killed by the hands
> of lawless men.
> But God raised him up,
> having loosed the pangs of death,
> because it was not possible for him
> to be held by it.
> (Acts 2:22–24)

NOTES

1. Roger Hazelton, *Christ and Ourselves: A Clue to Christian Life Today* (New York: Harper and Row Publishers, 1965), p. 111.

2. Wyn Blair Sutphin, *Thine the Glory* (New York: E. P. Dutton and Co., Inc., 1962), p. 15.

3. John Knox, *Chapters In A Life Of Paul* (Nashville: Abingdon-Cokesbury Press, 1950), p. 124.

Index

155